ARIZONA'S BEST GHOST TOWNS

ARIZONA'S BEST GHOST TOWNS

A Practical Guide by Philip Varney

Preface by Byrd Howell Granger • Maps and Drawings by G. E. Wolfe
Photographs by the Author

NORTHLAND PRESS • FLAGSTAFF, ARIZONA

Author/Photographer Philip Varney

for F. C. and Mary M. Varney

ISBN 0-87358-217-9 (cloth)
ISBN 0-87358-218-7 (paper)

Library of Congress Catalog Card Number 79-91724
Composed and Printed in the United States of America

CONTENTS

PREFACE

GHOST TOWN BUFFS and others who like to reach back in time to the solidity and ambience of the genuine and the old will delight in *Arizona's Best Ghost Towns: A Practical Guide*. It is more than a key to ghost towns, however, for it includes sites not associated with mining but nonetheless so interesting as to warrant their inclusion.

The practicality of this volume is immediately evident: the entries are grouped geographically rather than alphabetically. Further, Phil Varney has arranged them — with maps — in tours that make it possible for either the buff with time aplenty or the weekend explorer with limited hours to tackle sites as time dictates. And no person using this guide need drive toward a site only to discover too late that seasonal rains have made it impossible to reach. Using this book, travelers know before they go whether the family car, a four-wheel drive vehicle, or sound feet are required to complete the journey.

Getting there, of course, is only the beginning of the venture. Knowing ahead of time what to look for and what *can* be visited is one way to avoid keen disappointment. Unfortunately, some ghost town publications have pictures and information as out-of-date as hand wringers in a laundromat. But the photographs in this book were taken by the author within recent months. Furthermore, if a site is not worth a visit (unless one wishes to stand on the "place where"), Varney says so. And if a site exists and is worth seeing but is posted with "no trespassing" signs enforced by caretakers, the reader of this work will know it before setting out.

Armchair explorers will also find this book good reading. Varney is in love with his subject, and his devotion to it is revealed in his histories of locations, sometimes including legends, sometimes in delightful personal commentary. The result is that what could have been a dreary recitation of fact is actually a book to keep on the bedside table.

As I write this, I am struck by the fact that *Arizona's Best Ghost Towns: A Practical Guide* really does not need an introduction. Its title covers the subject. The book speaks clearly for itself.

BYRD HOWELL GRANGER

TO THE READER

ARIZONA'S BEST GHOST TOWNS has been written to fill a need, and the reader should know what this book does and does not attempt to do before he opens it for the first time while on the dusty road to Swansea in August.

This book does not attempt to cover all the tent camps and single-shaft overnight mines that are recorded in the history of Arizona; it focuses on the towns with the major remains. Secondly, it does not give a complete history of some sites; often only a paragraph or two of historical information appears. Finally, the book does not provide historical photographs reprinted from libraries and personal collections.

The book's full title, *Arizona's Best Ghost Towns: A Practical Guide* summarizes what I have attempted to do: I have written the book that I wanted to have with me on the seat of my truck as I headed toward the adventure of ghost town hunting. As a result, this book differs from others because it answers the questions I wanted answered before I began my journey:

- How much can I reasonably expect to see in a given period of time?
- What are the normal road conditions of the route?
- Do I need more than a road map and, if so, which map or maps should I buy?
- What is actually there at the site, *now,*

in the way of buildings, mines, or ruins?
- Which are the sites I really *must* see and which ones can I pass up if I don't have time to see them all?

To answer those questions, each chapter provides:

- a map of the area drawn to emphasize the towns and essential back roads
- individual entries containing current photographs, directions, history, and special points of interest
- a capsule summary of the sites in the chapter, ranking them in order as either "major," "secondary," or "minor" spots
- trip suggestions, including the time and mileage involved and the type of vehicle required
- a topographic map information chart, providing the names of the topos for the area and the degree to which each map is essential for finding and exploring the sites

All photographs are from the late 1970s, and most were taken in 1979. A gust of wind or a mindless vandal, however, can make a photograph instantly obsolete. Therefore, the photographs in this book show the prominent attractions of the sites, attractions that one can only hope will endure.

The appendixes cover topics that are related to ghost town hunting. Appendix A will help you learn to read topographic maps, an invaluable aid in finding some sites. If you don't know a mill from a smelter or an adit from a shaft, Appendix B is a primer of mining terms. Is it pronounced "suh-*loam*" or "suh-*loam*-ee"? Appendix C gives the correct pronunciation of towns and historical figures. In "Photographing Ghost Towns," Appendix D, are tips for successful photographs. And Appendix E, "Driving and Walking in Arizona," might help you avoid serious difficulties in Arizona's back country.

Here are some suggestions for successful ghost towning:

- Read the section in the book and study the maps before you go.
- Let someone know precisely where you're going.
- Talk to people in the towns: they know the best stories and can make the spots more personally memorable.
- Secure permission to visit spots when necessary. Often a friendly request will allow you to pass a "no trespassing" sign.
- Don't remove anything. ANYTHING. How would you feel if that rusted gate hinge had been removed by the person on the site just before you? (*Exception:* Why not remove a film wrapper or soft drink can, even if it's not yours?)
- Take a camera you're familiar with and plenty of film.
- Don't take a metal detector. It is frequently the badge of the vandal. Local residents dislike the device, and for good reasons.
- Collect ghost town books. One book's weakness is another's strength. A good place to start is:

Ghost Towns of Arizona, by James and Barbara Sherman (University of Oklahoma Press). The Shermans' book contains 130 entries, has detailed historical information, and is extremely informative. My book is a complement to, rather than a replacement of, this book.

ACKNOWLEDGMENTS

I wish to express my appreciation:

To Jim Sherman, whose book got me off the highway and onto the back roads; whose ghost town class and field trips have been informative and enjoyable; and whose suggestions and assistance have made this a better book. And to Jim and Barbara, grateful thanks for permission to use their book while writing mine.

To Dr. Byrd H. Granger, who more than anyone helped me to hone my writing skills and who encouraged and advised me on innumerable areas of this project. I deeply appreciate her permission to use *Arizona Place Names* in preparing this book.

To Freeman B. Hover, Tom Sanders, Allen McGinnis, William Broyles, Dorothy Kalil, Orval Northam, and Don Bufkin for reading and commenting on portions of the manuscript.

To trip companions Joseph H. Malone; Dick, Pauline, and Robert Upton; Tony and Betty Varney; and Freeman Hover and Al McGinnis, with special thanks to Al for the four-wheel drive vehicle.

To G. E. Wolfe, whose excellent maps and drawings add so much to each chapter.

To Tom Pagnozzi and Orval Northam for all their darkroom work and photographic advice.

To Mr. and Mrs. John McIntyre, for delighting my wife and me with stories and for making Sunnyside the special place it is.

To George P. Boone, for taking the time to give me the royal tour of Mineral Park.

To the late Mr. and Mrs. Ralph Morrow, who were so informative and gracious to my wife and me when we first met them at Hilltop in 1975. Our recent visit to the site was much emptier for their absence.

And finally, to my parents, Tony and Betty Varney, for proofreading and typing and retyping; and to my wife Marsha and my daughter Janet, for memorable ghost town trips together.

WHAT TO LOOK FOR AT GHOST TOWN SITES

WE ARE ALL SEARCHING for the ghost town with the body dangling from the hanging tree and the saloon door creaking with the wind. I suggest that you try a movie set. Unfortunately, often all that is left at a site is foundations or collapsed walls. Nevertheless, after a certain amount of practice you'll be able to see more than someone who isn't really looking.

Townsites where gold was found in the form of placer deposits, as in streams or streambeds, often have little remaining. Look for extensive disturbance of the stream itself and foundations right along the creek (see Big Bug and Placerita entries, pages 9 and 30).

Townsites where metals were extricated from the ground are usually much more rewarding than placer sites. The most obvious signs are adits and waste dumps on hillsides or shafts with headframes on more level spots. (See Appendix B, page 130, for definitions of these and following terms.) See the photograph of the Maxton Mine for a good example of an adit (page 10), the photographs for the Snyder Mine and Vulture entries for headframes (pages 79 and 24), and McMillanville (page 71) for a picture of a waste dump.

Mine buildings or their foundations usually last longer than the towns they supported, since the structures were of much heavier construction and were more difficult to move. Mills, even after they have been dismantled or destroyed, are often still prominent since they are usually built into sides of hills to use the assistance of gravity. Good examples of mill foundations can be found at Venezia, Signal, and Cerro Colorado, among others (for a photograph, see Columbia, page 62). A mill itself is easy to spot since it will have a roof line that slopes or "steps down" from the top of the hill. Perhaps the best surviving mill in Arizona is at Cerbat (see photograph, page 50). The concrete remains of another good mill is at Copper Hill (see photograph, page 72).

A smelter is a heavy-duty building. If it has not been demolished for salvage (this has often happened, particularly during World War II), it should stand for generations; however, although most mining towns had mills, relatively few had smelters. See photographs of Swansea, Clarkdale, and Humboldt for fairly extensive remains (pages 44, 6, and 12). See Sasco for an example of a dismantled smelter with only foundations remaining (page 76).

One of the most enduring remains of a ghost town is a railroad bed. In fact, the current road to the town is often an old bed. The roads to Sasco, Crown King, and Poland are good examples.

Rock and mortar buildings tend to last in Arizona better than others (see photographs of Sasco and Mowry, pages 76 and 99). Brick is often carted away, and wood is used for buildings in nearby towns or, unhappily, for fires. Adobe can last for centuries *if* it has a roof. When the roof collapses on an adobe structure, the building will deteriorate rapidly. The adobe houses at Salero, built in the 1880s, still have roofs and are quite habitable. A few miles north is the adobe Alto Post Office, which was built in 1907 but has no roof. There the adobe crumbles with each rain (see photographs on pages 80 and 82).

Generally speaking, the best ghost towns are the ones most closely watched. Swansea, abandoned and remote, has been burned, carved, and exhumed. Sunnyside, near popular Parker Canyon Lake, has survived because it has caretakers. And one of the best of them all, Vulture, is carefully supervised and even has an admission charge. My advice is that, instead of muttering to yourself when forking over your dollar, you thank the owners: if they weren't there, more than likely the town wouldn't be, either.

But don't stop looking for that elusive ghost town with the playing cards still on the table. I found it — once. But I won't hand it to you — read the entries to find out where.

A WORD OF CAUTION ABOUT DIRECTIONS AND MAPS

EACH ENTRY BEGINS with explicit directions that were accurate when the site was last visited. Of course, over the years changes can occur: a new road could bypass the site; a locked gate could be put across the only access; or, tragically, an entire site could be razed or burned.

The maps accompanying this book are not intended to replace topographic maps when sites are far from main roads. The maps are intended to give a clear picture of the towns' positions relative to main roads, larger towns, and other ghost town sites. The reader will need to use the maps in conjunction with the directions for each entry and occasionally with one or more topographic maps. At the end of each chapter is a Topographic Map Information page that tells the reader which maps are essential.

MAP LEGEND

⊛ MAJOR SITE
✪ Secondary Site
○ MINOR SITE
◯ NON-GHOSTS

━ ━ ━ MAJOR HIGHWAY
▨▨▨ Paved Road
⌇⌇⌇ Unpaved Road

Areas of Arizona Covered by the Chapters

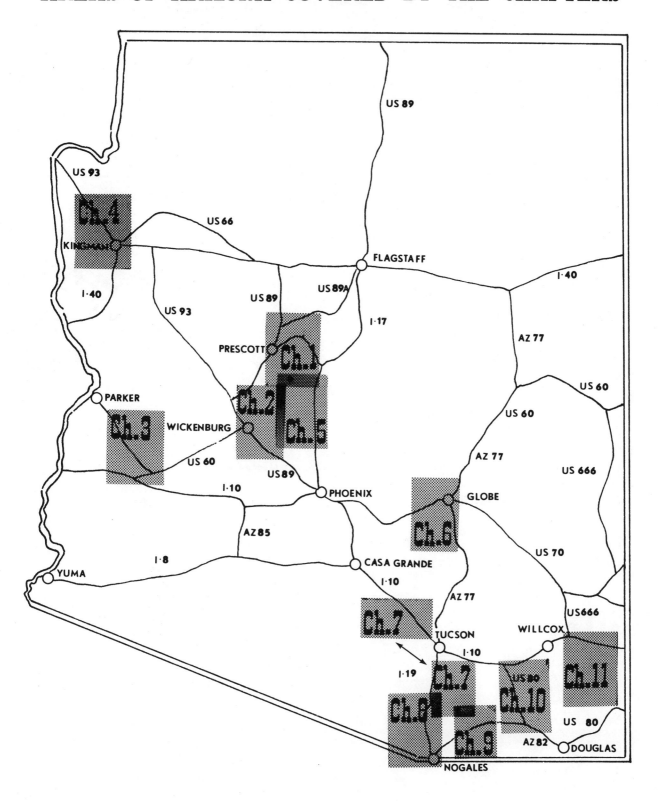

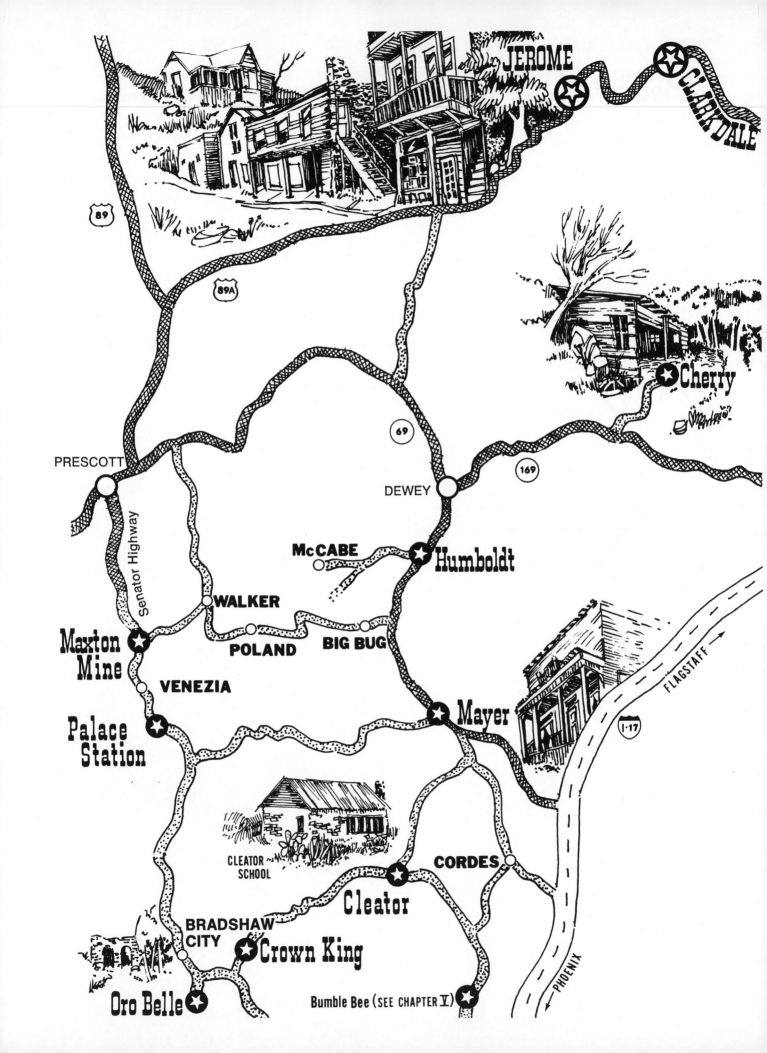

JEROME

CLARKDALE

89

89A

Cherry

69

169

PRESCOTT

DEWEY

McCABE

Humboldt

Senator Highway

WALKER

Maxton
Mine

POLAND

BIG BUG

VENEZIA

Mayer

FLAGSTAFF

I-17

Palace
Station

CLEATOR
SCHOOL

CORDES

Cleator

BRADSHAW
CITY

Crown King

PHOENIX

Oro Belle

Bumble Bee (SEE CHAPTER V)

CHAPTER ONE

NEAR PRESCOTT · GHOSTS OF THE HIGHER GROUND

Prescott, 96 miles north of Phoenix and 60 miles north of Wickenburg, is one of Arizona's most beautiful and enjoyable towns. As a "mile high" city, it features much milder summers than most of Arizona, yet its winters are not nearly as severe as higher elevation towns like Flagstaff. Founded in 1864 and named for historian William H. Prescott, the town served as the first capital of the Arizona Territory.

Prescott contains some of the most elegant examples in the state of architecture of the 1880s–1920s, so you should not merely use Prescott as a base of departure for outlying sites. Instead, you should become familiar with the Victorian homes, the handsome stores, and the wonderful courthouse square with its bandshell and famous equestrian statue of Rough Rider Buckey O'Neill.

The logical place to learn about Prescott is at the Sharlot Hall Museum, three blocks west of the courthouse square on Gurley Street, where one can see exhibits about the area and tour the original governor's mansion. While there, obtain an informative brochure on Victorian and Historic Buildings of Prescott. This brochure contains a self-guided tour map of the town. For the ghost town hunter, an important street in Prescott is South Mt. Vernon, because it leads directly into the Senator Highway, which is the former stage route going to Maxton and points south.

JEROME

Jerome is 33 miles northeast of Prescott on U.S. 89A.

Jerome comes upon you in an instant as you drive from Prescott. At one moment you're progressing through a series of switchbacks on a pine-studded mountain, and at the next turn you suddenly have it all before you: dozens and dozens of buildings — some up there with you, some fifteen hundred feet below you — all clinging to a thirty percent slope.

When you are coming from the east from Phoenix and Flagstaff, the view is less startling, since you can see Jerome from miles away. But it is no less awesome. It begins as a mere glint of tin roofs and a tiny "J" on a mountainside, but as you get closer, the size of the town becomes more apparent. From either direction, you'll wonder why the town isn't sliding downhill. It is. Jerome sits upon the Verde Fault and has eighty miles of tunnels undermining it. The movement of the town has been gradual but inexorable since a mighty dynamite blast was set off underground in 1925. Since then, Jerome's famous Traveling Jail has slid about three hundred feet, and some houses have moved at the rate of four inches per year. Residents seem unconcerned: there is the possibly apocryphal tale of the night the movie theater slipped two feet.

Jerome on Cleopatra Hill: the houses at the top were mine officials' residences; below the buildings of the central business district is the famous "traveling jail"; at the bottom of the photograph is the Methodist Church, now a private residence.

During all the quivering and shaking, the projector whirred on and the audience watched the film with frozen attention. After all, the movie was the only exciting thing happening in town.

Indians used the colorful Jerome azurite for facial decorations and pottery tinting over one thousand years ago. Spaniards in the sixteenth century examined the minerals in the area and went on, since what they wanted was gold. Jerome's modern era began in 1876. A claim filed by M. A. Ruffner and Angus McKinnon, eventually to be worth $500 million, was sold for $40,000 to an eastern concern, which in turn sold out to Arizona's Territorial Governor F. A. Tritle. In 1882, Tritle formed the United Verde Company with two other men, one of whom was Eugene Jerome,

who said he would join on the condition that the town be named after him.

Jerome became a boom town after Montana millionaire and U.S. Senator William A. Clark bought out the United Verde in 1888. By 1899 the town was the fourth largest city in the Arizona Territory, featuring a hospital, schools, hotels, churches, saloons, and such refinements as electric lights, a railroad, two newspapers, and stylish Victorian homes for mining officials.

But there was a price for the prosperity. Smoke from the smelter was so acrid that all vegetation died on Cleopatra Hill, including oak and pine trees. People gagged on the toxic sulfurous fumes. Buildings occasionally collapsed due to the constant blasting. And despite Senator Clark's efforts

Above: Once a mine official's house, this now looks like the epitome of the ghost town haunted house.

Below: Clarkdale — Barrigan's Bar in Patio Town. Jerome is in the background.

The Little Daisy Hotel, built in the 1920s

to improve conditions, the mines and smelter were scenes of frequent accidents and deaths.

In 1916 a rival to the United Verde Copper Company named the United Verde Extension Mining Company (UVX) hit an incredibly rich copper body worth $125 million at a mine called the Little Daisy just north of town. One of the owners, James S. Douglas, built a white mansion adjacent to the

The Hotel Connor and the Liberty Theater, at the center of Jerome's business district

mine in the 1920s and also constructed a modern hotel, named the Little Daisy in honor of the mine, just west of the main shaft.

The Great Depression could have brought an end to the glory of Jerome. But in 1935, Phelps Dodge bought out both the United Verde and the UVX for $35 million in what was regarded by some as a very unwise move considering the perilous financial climate of the day. Within only five years, however, Phelps Dodge had shown a profit of $40 million. The company finally shut down operations in 1953, and in the same year at a mass town meeting the Jerome Historical Society was formed to help preserve and maintain the dramatic remains of one of America's great mineral finds: over a period of sixty-five years, between $800 million and one billion dollars in copper and other precious metals was extracted from the slopes of Cleopatra Hill.

Today, the Jerome Historical Society operates a museum out of the former Fashion Saloon in the center of town. North of the town itself, at the James S. Douglas mansion, the State of Arizona runs a second museum. Both are very worthwhile and are good places to start your tour of the city.

Jerome avoids the flagrant tourist-mecca approach of some other ghost towns, but the merchants still help to keep the town alive, so I like

Note the graceful stone arches and the ornamental tin on the column of this elegant building on Jerome's main street.

to patronize the shops or at least thank an owner occasionally for preserving his corner of Jerome. You will find antique stores, a gourmet restaurant, and crafts and gift shops in the center of town. There is also a well-conceived town-within-a-building at The Schoolhouse, a converted elementary school.

Noncommercial attractions abound, and it would be hopeless to try to list them all. But some of my favorite spots include the red brick Holy Family Catholic Church and the Victorian company homes farther up the same street; the Methodist Church, built between 1939 and 1941 out of old powder boxes and mining timbers; and the Little Daisy Hotel and the Douglas mansion, on the same road beyond the church. You also shouldn't miss the often-overlooked Jerome Cemetery. Where the main road hairpins past the former high school, take the dirt road heading north. The

cemetery offers a beautiful view of Jerome, and the stones and markers give testimony to the universality of the lure of mineral wealth: natives of Italy, Germany, Russia, and Ireland are buried there.

CLARKDALE

Clarkdale is 5 miles northeast of Jerome on U.S. 89A.

Clarkdale, built in 1912 by Jerome's William Clark as a model company town and smelter, might be Arizona's most overlooked ghost town. Residents will take issue with calling their town a ghost, and they are partially right. Clarkdale is a pleasant community with many well-kept former company houses and a beautiful view. But along with the living are the dead. On the east end of town, mixed in with the attractively refurbished com-

Above: The remains of the Clarkdale smelter

Below: The Crown King Saloon (see entry, page 16)

pany houses are occasional dilapidated, empty ones. North of town is the huge skeleton of what was dubbed "the most modern smelter in the world" when it was erected in 1912.

Southeast of the smelter is the partially occupied Patio Town, the area originally "reserved" for Clarkdale's Mexican-American population. Clarkdale was almost totally segregated, apparently by mutual consent: even in the early 1960s when an Anglo family moved into the building that had been the Mexicans' dance hall, some older Mexicans objected to the intrusion into "their" part of town, although the feeling was not generally shared by the younger generation. Next door to the dance hall still stands what was once the favorite watering hole, Barrigan's Bar, which apparently had a bookie operation in the basement. That must have required a certain amount of gall, for not twenty yards to the north still sits the now-abandoned Clarkdale jail.

CHERRY

Cherry is 32 miles east of Prescott and 15 miles east of Dewey on Arizona 169. (The route from Dewey to Cherry is excellent. The northern route from Arizona 279 to Cherry is narrow and through mountainous terrain and not recommended for passenger vehicles.)

Cherry was named for the abundance of wild cherry trees lining Cherry Creek's canyons, although some confusion as to the origin of the name has since occurred because the Norville Cherry family moved to the area from Texas several years after the naming of the community. The post office was established in 1884, but mines had already been operating in the district for many years by then. In 1907, six mills were at work crushing the gold-rich ore.

Today, Cherry is a quiet community with a few occupied houses, an occasional abandoned structure, and the pleasant Cherry Creek Antique Store. One house on the main road is the former Cherry School. A stage stop/residence dating from about 1865 originally stood a mile east of town; now the building is being carefully restored and is 200 yards from its original site. Approximately 150 yards west of the antique store is the manza-

Residence and stage stop from the 1860s, now being restored

The Cherry schoolhouse, now a private residence

nita-filled Cherry cemetery. A road about 0.6 miles west of town heads north 1 mile to the Gold Bullion Mine, which features a beautiful, gravity feed mill of weathered wood. You should secure permission to enter the premises.

Remains of many mines dot the Cherry area; the Mingus Mountain 1944 15' map is helpful in locating them.

The mill of the Gold Bullion Mine, northwest of Cherry

WALKER

Walker is 12 miles southeast of Prescott. Take Arizona 69 to the Walker turnoff and head south.

In 1863, Captain Joseph Reddeford Walker led a party of thirty-four gold seekers into the territory of the Yavapai Indians. The trek began in New Mexico, proceeded to Tucson, and finally ended up following the Hassayampa River north. Walker, who served with Kit Carson and who had previously led a party from the Great Salt Lake to California, was sixty-five when he and his followers found gold along a river called Ookilsipava by the Indians. The creek was renamed when Sam Miller found a lynx lying in the water, and taking it for dead, leaned down to pick it up. It sprang up and wounded Sam, who in a fit of rage kicked the animal to death. Ever since it has been known as Lynx Creek.

Walker — an abandoned remnant

The town of Walker developed along Lynx Creek. The population during the initial rush to the area rose to over 2,000, but by the time the community received a post office in 1879, the population was a mere 150. A fire in 1909 destroyed most of the permanent buildings of Walker.

Today the townsite of Walker is marked only by a Forest Service sign, although a wood building and foundations are 0.3 miles along the road past the sign. Beyond the wood building 0.2 miles, the road crosses the rubble of the Poland-Walker tunnel, completed in 1904 but now caved in at the Walker end. A scant foundation of what might have been a mill or smelter can be seen 1 mile south of the Walker sign. Fred Williams's Potato Patch, which was the food basket of the area, is 3 miles south of Walker, and the site of Maxton is 1 mile farther south.

The principal attraction at Walker today is an often-overlooked charcoal kiln. Although not in as dramatic a setting as the five coke ovens at Cochran (see page 69), this 1880s kiln is well worth visiting and considerably easier to reach than those

Kiln at Walker. Wood was dropped through a hole near the top of the back, and the large door was sealed. Charcoal was removed after the intense heating process was complete.

at Cochran. From the Walker townsite Forest Service sign, take the road to Big Bug Mesa for 0.7 miles. Turn down a road to the right and proceed for 0.2 miles. Park your car at the turnaround and take a two-minute walk down an obvious trail to the kiln.

BIG BUG

Big Bug is 4.1 miles north of Mayer. Turn west at Poland Junction and continue on the main road for 1.8 miles, where you will see tailings opposite you on the northern hillside. Park your car and go down to the riverbed to the south.

Big Bug Creek, named by miners from Walker in 1863 for the enormous beetles still found in the area today, was worked for gold beginning in the 1880s and culminating with dredging operations in the 1890s. The only remains of the community of Big Bug, which had a post office from 1879 to 1910 and a peak population of around a hundred,

is the scarred hillside to the north and the upturned streambed of Big Bug Creek. The piles of stone sometimes reach heights of fifteen feet, and the evidence of the operation extends for miles along the creek to the south.

Mining in Big Bug was spearheaded by Theodore Boggs, great-grandson of Daniel Boone and son of Missouri's Governor Lilburn W. Boggs, a relentless persecutor of Mormons in the 1840s. Theodore Boggs came to Arizona in 1862 and worked the Big Bug claim. A few miles to the south of Big Bug was Boggs Smelter, where over a million dollars' worth of precious metal was smelted.

POLAND

Poland Junction is 4 miles south of Humboldt on Arizona 69. Poland itself is 8 miles west of the junction.

Summer cottages and homes in an area called Breezy Pines now occupy the former town of Poland. The community was founded in 1872 as a result of the silver discoveries made by Davis Robert Poland.

Retaining walls, perhaps of the mill, at Poland

The real prosperity of Poland began around the turn of the century when Frank M. Murphy and his associates financed the digging of the 8,017-foot tunnel to Walker. This enabled ore to be sent from the Sheldon Mine at Walker through the tunnel by mule train to be shipped by a branch line of the Prescott-Crown King Railroad down to Poland Junction, where it joined the main line.

The mouth of the Poland-Walker tunnel at the Poland end

Adit of the Maxton Mine, visible across the ravine from the Senator Highway

The mill shut down in 1913, and the post office closed the same year.

Mill foundations and rock retaining walls are evident on the north side of the road entering Poland. A road veering back to the northeast, 8.1 miles west of Poland Junction, proceeds up to the most interesting spot at the townsite: the eastern mouth of the Poland-Walker tunnel. Unless you have four-wheel drive, leave your car at the foot of the hill and walk the short distance to the tunnel.

MAXTON

Maxton is 4 miles south of Walker and 4.5 miles south of Groom Creek on the Senator Highway.

Remains of Maxton and Senator — waste dumps, foundations, adits, and tailings — line the Hassayampa River. The most obvious remnant of the area is the Maxton Mine, on the south side of the Hassayampa, with its ore tracks still leading into the mine and its tin building still standing at the mine's entrance. Across the river are the steel girders of a mill from a much later era than the boom years of the 1870s to the 1890s. Farther south 0.5 miles, almost to the big switchback to Walker, are the concrete steps and foundation of the post office and store of "Max" Alwens, after whom Maxton was named.

The steps of Max Alwens's store and post office lead up only to foundations.

VENEZIA

Venezia is 16 miles southeast of Prescott and 1.3 miles north of Palace Station.

Venezia, Goodwin, and Maxton — three sites separated by eight miles — shared a post office, which moved among the three towns. The progress of its relocation sounds like a double play: Goodwin (1894) to Maxton (1901) to Venezia (1916) to Goodwin (1935). The only remnants of a town are in Venezia, where concrete foundations of a mill are just over a rise on the northeast side of the road. A lifelong resident of the community said that the town's dilapidated buildings, which stood southeast of the mill and across the creek, were torn down a few years ago because they were dangerous to visitors. Without those buildings, there will be very few visitors and little danger. The lone remains at the townsite are scattered rubble, a picked-over dump, and a bench seat between two trees.

Venezia was apparently named by an Italian immigrant in honor of Venice, his native city. Goodwin, named for Territorial Governor John W. Goodwin, once stood three miles south of Venezia but has vanished completely.

PALACE STATION

Palace Station is 17 miles south of Prescott and 1.3 miles south of Venezia on the Senator Highway.

A. B. Spence built the Palace Station in 1874 as a home for his family and a rest stop for travelers on the stage line between Phoenix and Prescott near what then was known as Spence Spring. Miners in the area used the Palace Station as the place to congregate and swap lies after a day's labor at their claims. It served as a stage station until 1910.

Today the Palace Station, one of the state's oldest buildings constructed by white men, is used by Forest Service employees. The Forest Service has carefully preserved and protected the cabin and the modest cemetery 50 yards to the northeast. The site is an attraction for the ghost town enthusiast not because of the extensive remains in the area but rather for this quaint and beautiful cabin: Palace Station provides a glimpse into the frontier past in an authentic and unassuming way.

Palace Station, a stage stop and residence built by A. B. Spence

HUMBOLDT

Humboldt is 19 miles east of Prescott and 8 miles north of Mayer on Arizona 69.

The only stack remaining from Humboldt's days as the principal smelter town of Yavapai County

Humboldt is a good example of the effect of the on-again, off-again mining industry upon a small community. Now a quiet town situated in the pleasant Agua Fria Valley, Humboldt was first settled in the 1860s, flourished between 1898 and 1918, was deserted in the early 1920s, prospered again in the 1930s, and finally settled into its present peaceful repose after 1969.

The town was originally called Val Verde for the smelter of the same name at the site. Humboldt, under which name the post office was opened in 1905, was chosen in honor of the German geographer and explorer Baron Alexander Von Humboldt, who had toured Mexico in the late 1700s and had predicted that the region now called Arizona, then Pimería Alta, would be the location of great mineral wealth.

Although mining activity did take place near the town, Humboldt's first major activity resulted from the smelters constructed there to process the ore for two copper and lead mines, the Blue Bell and the DeSoto, fifteen miles away in the Bradshaw Mountains. The Prescott and Eastern Railroad, a branch of the Santa Fe, brought the ore up from the mines to the smelters. The DeSoto is south of Cleator, and part of the tramway from the mine to the railroad is still visible on the hill to the west of the road from Cleator to Crown King (see page 16).

The mines and smelters prospered through the end of World War I, but the town was absolutely deserted by 1924. Humboldt briefly came back to life in the late 1920s, but in 1935 it was a ghost town once again. The town's most enduring prosperity began in 1934 when Fred Gibbs, now of Prescott, acquired the Iron King mine, only 0.5 miles southwest of town. The Iron King produced over $100 million in lead and zinc before closing in 1968.

Humboldt false-front store;
note the angled front door.

Today, one stack remains from the smelter operations. The old stack, erected in 1889, was toppled in 1955 because it was deemed a hazard; on that day school was recessed so that the whole town could watch it go. Main Street in Humboldt features several historic buildings, including the Bank of Humboldt, which now houses a Catholic church. Other buildings, including wooden false fronts, are on Humboldt's back streets. You can also drive up to the Iron King to see the mine, although it is still operating on a limited scale producing Ironite, a soil additive.

An article about the boom or bust nature of Humboldt that appeared in 1926 in a periodical called the *Silver Belt* issued a warning that could have been given to most of the towns in this book:

Another lesson to be learned from the experience of Humboldt is that any community should strive earnestly and consistently to work itself out of a situation wherein its commercial and industrial existence is entirely dependent upon a single industry.

Humboldt gas station, with pumps from two eras

McCABE

At the south end of Humboldt on Arizona 69 is a road heading west to the Iron King Mine. Take this road past the mine buildings and head west on the dirt road that drops down from the mine site. Keep on this road until it branches; then take the right fork. You will know you're on the correct road when you are driving in what in reality is a wash. On the right, about 1 mile from the fork in the road, is the McCabe cemetery. From the cemetery, take the left fork into the western part of the townsite. Park your truck here and walk farther east across the wash. You will come to scattered brick and wood ruins.

The best of the very modest remains at McCabe:
the cemetery

The White House Hotel at Mayer: double porches exhibit antique furniture and implements.

*The Mayer Hotel, built in 1889, is still a showplace.
It is currently being carefully refurbished.*

The porch of the Mayer Hotel

McCabe is now a very minor ghost in the foothills of the Bradshaw Mountains. A tiny cemetery, hundreds of broken bricks (I did not see *one* whole one), rusted tin, and some wood debris are all that remain at the townsite. Mine and mill evidence are on the hillside.

In 1883, Frank McCabe discovered gold at the site, and by 1898 the town of McCabe had a post office, stage service to Prescott and Phoenix, and a population of several hundred. The mine closed in 1913, and the post office was discontinued in 1917.

MAYER

Mayer is 28 miles southeast of Prescott and 8 miles west of I-17 from the Cordes Junction exit.

Although Mayer is not a ghost town, you should not simply consider it a place to drive through on the way to Cordes, Cleator, and Crown King, because the town contains several attractive buildings dating from the late 1880s. Joe Mayer founded the town in 1881, which then featured his store, his saloon, and a stage station. Farmers and miners in the area made the community a popular trade center. In 1889, Joe Mayer built the Mayer Hotel, a two-story wooden building on Main Street that is the principal attraction of the Mayer business center. To the east is the Mayer State Bank, now a private residence. To the west of the hotel are two red brick buildings that were once the town's brothels.

Former brothel next door to the Mayer Hotel

Also on Main Street, east of the town's center, is the two-story, brick White House Hotel, built in 1903 and open to guests until 1977. The White House features attractive full-length porches on both floors. Mining and farming equipment decorate the side yard, and in a garage at the rear are several vintage automobiles clearly marked "Not for Sale."

Mayer's most noticeable landmark is the smelter stack on Highway 69 on the north side of town.

CORDES

Cordes is 7.1 miles from Mayer. Take the dirt road on the southeastern edge of Mayer that heads south. About 1.2 miles from Mayer the road branches, but you should take the main road, which goes to the left.

John Henry Cordes named this small settlement for his family when he became postmaster in 1886. Previously, the site had been known as Antelope Station because it was located on Antelope Creek.

The gas station at Cordes

The post office ceased operation in 1944. The community was still active until the mid-1950s, when the Black Canyon Highway bypassed the town by three miles.

A principal building of interest in Cordes is the old gas station, built in 1915 and closed in 1973, on the west side of the road at the town's only intersection. Old cars and trucks and assorted parts lie rusting near the station. To the east of the station is a barn built in 1912, and the Cordes home, which was constructed in 1875. The Cordes family still owns the property.

CLEATOR

Cleator is 7 miles southwest of Cordes. Drive south from Cordes about 2.5 miles. Take the right fork (the left goes to Bumble Bee) and continue for 4.5 more miles.

Turkey Creek, which runs north of the town of Cleator, provided the original name for this settlement on the eastern slopes of the Bradshaws. The Turkey Creek Mining District was organized in 1864, which makes the area one of the earliest settlements in Yavapai County. In addition to being the center of commerce for nearby mines, Turkey Creek (also known as Turkey and Turkey Creek Station) was located on a branch of the Prescott and Eastern Railroad, built principally by Chinese laborers in 1902, which connected the mines at Crown King to the towns of Mayer and Prescott.

The name was changed to Cleator in 1925 by James P. Cleator, who had arrived in Turkey Creek twenty years before and who eventually owned most of the town. The railroad line was abandoned in 1933; in 1949, Mr. Cleator tried in vain to sell his town. The post office was closed in 1954, and James Cleator died in 1959.

*Cleator, at the foot of the Bradshaws. To the immediate left is the schoolhouse;
on the road beyond the school is the Cleator store.*

Today, Cleator consists of about a dozen residences, a vacant WPA-built stone schoolhouse, and the Cleator General Store, an antique that dates back to the days when it was the Turkey General Store. It now has several additions attached to the original structure. The schoolhouse, just north of the store, offers the photographer and artist a picturesque and stately subject.

South of Cleator 2.5 miles is the site of the town of Middleton, which was the point on the railroad at which ore was delivered from the DeSoto Mine high on the mountain to the west. A four-thousand-foot tramway, parts of which are still clearly visible, brought the ore from mine to train.

The Cleator General Store

CROWN KING

Crown King is 13 miles south of Cleator and 55 miles southeast of Prescott.

The well-maintained mountain road from Cleator to Crown King, with all its hairpins and switchbacks, was originally the roadbed of a branch line of the Prescott and Eastern Railroad, constructed by Chinese laborers just after the turn of the century. The trains filled with ore would ease forward down the mountain grade, head into a switchback,

The WPA-built school in Cleator

back down to the next switchback, and then ease down again. As you travel through the hairpins, notice that at each sharp turn there is a place where the railroad would go past, reverse the switch, and then continue down. Watch also for the DeSoto, the Peck, and the Swastika mines high above you to the west.

Mill foundations are on the left-hand side as you enter the area of Crown King from the northeast. The town's center of activity is the Crown King General Store, in operation for about a hundred years. Next door is Crown King's saloon, which looks just the way saloons are pictured in the western movies. This particular saloon was brought by pack mules, piece by piece, from Oro Belle, five miles away, in about 1910.

After you have walked around the area of the general store, take the road heading north that parallels the road you came in on but is on the opposite side of the creek. Veer up to the left at the first intersection and then left again to visit the Crown King school. Then continue on the same road, past several interesting residences, until you come to the intersection of Moss and Tower, 0.6 miles from the general store. Tower Street continues to the Crown King Mine, and Moss heads toward the isolated and picturesque Crown King Cemetery, the turnoff to which is 0.3 miles up Moss Road. Take the sharp right turn for a short drive or

walk over to the cemetery's beautifully-crafted iron fence.

When the Crowned King gold mine was discovered in the 1870s, it was thought to be the biggest strike of what was being called the "Bradshaw Excitement." The rock in which the gold was found, however, proved to be very uncooperative for the milling and smelting methods of the day. In the late 1880s, the Crowned King Mining Company, with Illinois banker George P. Harrington as part owner, began to make a series of discoveries that brought genuine prosperity to the

Deserted but habitable home on a back road through Crown King

The Crown King School

Oro Belle — the Tiger Gold Company Store

area. By the end of 1888 the camp, its name now shortened to Crown King, had five hundred buildings. A post office, with George Harrington as postmaster, opened the same year. Within ten years the town had electric lights and one telephone.

By the turn of the century, the Crowned King had produced over $1.5 million in gold, but disputes within the ownership brought lawsuits and countersuits that closed the mine. George Harrington left the operation and turned his energies to his holdings at the Oro Belle Mine and the town of Harrington, later known as Oro Belle.

The railroad reached Crown King in 1904, but the Crowned King Mine's best days were almost over. Various owners tried to rework waste dumps and develop the mine further, but the town slowly slipped into what it is today — a charming community of summer homes and cabins.

ORO BELLE

Oro Belle is 5 miles southwest of Crown King. Take the main road south from Crown King, head west at the fork 0.5 miles from town, and take the road heading south about 1 mile farther on. This is not a passenger car road, but I made it without serious difficulty with a two-wheel drive truck. Oro Belle is 3 miles south on this road.

Although Oro Belle only contains three dilapidated buildings, it still is one of my favorite ghost towns. The site is completely abandoned and is remote enough to virtually guarantee solitude, and it features just enough remains to entice the visitor to look farther up this trail or across that canyon.

George B. Harrington organized the Oro Belle (Spanish-French: "beautiful gold") Mining District in the late 1890s. The town itself, then known as Harrington, had a peak population of about 200, a mill, saloons, and various other buildings. The Oro Belle, the Savoy, and the Rapid Transit were the principal mines in the area. Some confusion exists about post offices. According to *Arizona Place Names,* the town of Harrington was near the Oro Bell (*sic*) Mine and had a post office from 1904 to 1918. But the same source also says that the town of Oro, at a slightly different location, was the post office for the Oro Belle Mine from 1904 to 1907. At any rate, the mines played out around 1910, and parts of Oro Belle were transported to nearby Crown King, including the saloon that is still open for business there.

An old photograph of Oro Belle hanging in the Crown King Saloon shows fourteen buildings, including a large mill along with several tents. Today, some traces of the mill still exist west of the remaining tin buildings, both of which are collapsing. The roofless rock structure east of the tin buildings was once two stories high. The back of a sheet of ornamental tin from that structure reads "Tiger Gold Co. Store." George Harrington's mining operation was called the Tiger Gold Company, and the Tiger Mine was about 2 miles north of Oro Belle. Several water tanks are in the area, and at the Oro Belle Mine above the townsite are shacks, remains of mining equipment, and waste dumps.

For much of my tour of Oro Belle, I was accompanied by a stray kitten as abandoned as the townsite, who shared lunch with me and my companions and purred contentedly most of the way back to Prescott. She no longer lives in a ghost town, but her name, of course, is Oro Belle.

The site of Bradshaw City

BRADSHAW CITY

Bradshaw City is 0.2 miles west of the turnoff to Oro Belle on the Senator Highway.

Nothing but a Forest Service sign marking the site remains at Bradshaw City, a town created in 1871 to serve the needs of the silver-rich Tiger Mine to the south. The town's prosperity lasted less than a year, and when a post office opened in 1874, the town was already in a state of decline. The town's population had deserted the area by the mid-1880s.

Bradshaw City and the mountain range of the same name honor William D. Bradshaw, who with his brother Isaac made rich discoveries in the area

in 1863, several months after Captain Walker's party found gold near Prescott. Bradshaw was a heavy drinker and cut his throat with a razor during a fit of delirium tremens at the town of La Paz in Yuma County. He is buried there in an unmarked grave.

The only vestige left of the town is the Bradshaw City Cemetery, reached by taking the road to Oro Belle for 0.5 miles and then heading west on a five-minute walk along a definite trail. Not much of the cemetery remains, but the overlook from the nearby rocks is breathtaking. The most noticeable manmade feature of the view is the Tiger Mine, 0.5 miles to the south.

CAPSULE SUMMARY

(In order of importance of sites)

MAJOR SITES

Jerome and Clarkdale — the most extensive, most dramatic ghost towns in Arizona

SECONDARY SITES

Crown King — quiet summer resort with historic buildings and a cemetery

Cherry — a few buildings in a peaceful spot

Mayer — two outstanding hotels in a non-ghost town

Humboldt — a smelter stack, mine, and several good buildings

Cleator — a school, a store, and several residences

Oro Belle — three ruins of buildings in a remote, beautiful spot

Palace Station — only one log cabin, but special

Maxton — a mine in a dramatic setting

MINOR SITES

Walker — one building, some foundations, and a charcoal kiln

Poland — a tunnel entrance and a mill foundation

McCabe — a cemetery and rubble

Cordes — a good service station

Big Bug — no buildings, but extensive dredging evidence

Bradshaw City — sparse remnants of a cemetery

Venezia — mill foundation and rubble

TRIP SUGGESTIONS

Warning: Do not drive to Prescott on a summer weekend assuming you will find lodgings. Although there are hundreds of motel rooms, Prescott is a favorite weekend retreat from Phoenix's summer heat, so advance reservations are advisable.

Here are ten suggestions for trips to the many towns in the Prescott area. Each summary includes towns, approximate distances and time required for the round trip from Prescott, approximate time to allow for, and the type of vehicle required.

TRIP 1: Jerome and Clarkdale

Jerome is the most dramatic ghost town in Arizona and possibly in the nation; no enthusiast should miss it. Clarkdale, a semi-ghost, has many good "company town" buildings. This passenger car trip will cover approximately 75 miles of mountain driving on paved roads. Stay a half day or all day, depending upon your desire to prowl these two rewarding towns.

TRIP 1A: Jerome, Clarkdale, and Cherry

Adding Cherry, a quiet and scenic rural ghost, creates an all-day loop trip from and to Prescott and adds about 50 miles. The road to Cherry is

unpaved but easily passable for a passenger car if you come into town from Arizona 169.

TRIP 2: Walker, Big Bug, and Poland

In 1904, an 8,000-foot tunnel, now sealed off at the western entrance, was completed to connect Walker and Poland. By taking an 82-mile passenger car trip you can visit the towns at either end. Although they are minor sites, both are in very picturesque country. Big Bug is interesting, not for buildings but for the remains of the dredging operations of Big Bug Creek. Plan to take four to five hours for the whole trip.

Note: A rough road suitable for jeeps crosses from Walker to Poland. Consult the Groom Creek 7½′ topographic map.

TRIP 3: Maxton, Venezia, and Palace Station

This 3-hour 34-mile truck trip goes to an abandoned mine, a vanished town, and a delightful cabin. Exploring Maxton thoroughly requires a great deal of climbing and extreme caution. You can continue past Palace Station down the Senator Highway to Crown King (see trip 6c).

TRIP 4: Humboldt and McCabe

Humboldt, although not a ghost, has many good buildings, an abandoned smelter, and the Iron King Mine. For the 6-mile drive to McCabe, a dilapidated minor ghost town, a truck or four-wheel drive vehicle is required. This 52-mile round trip excursion takes three to four hours.

TRIP 5: Cherry, Humboldt, and Mayer

Mayer, not a ghost town, has many charming buildings worth examining. See trips 4 and 1a for Humboldt and Cherry. This 84-mile passenger car trip requires four to five hours.

TRIP 6: Mayer, Cordes, Cleator, and Bumble Bee

Mayer and Cordes both contain good period buildings. Cleator and Bumble Bee (see page 62) are small ghost towns, each with its own attractions. Five or six hours are necessary for this passenger car trip of 96 miles, 52 miles of which are on pavement.

TRIP 6A: Add Crown King to Trip 6

Crown King is a pleasant summer community and

old mining town 13 miles from Cleator on an old railroad bed. The terrain is fairly mountainous but the road is passable for a passenger car. Add three hours to trip 6. You might consider dropping Bumble Bee from trip 6 if you add Crown King.

TRIP 6B: Mayer, Cordes, Cleator, Crown King, Bradshaw City, and Oro Belle

The addition of Oro Belle necessitates either a truck or a four-wheel drive vehicle and about three extra hours, even though Oro Belle is only 5 miles from Crown King. The town is an abandoned ghost with three collapsed buildings and mine ruins. On the road to Oro Belle is the Bradshaw City Cemetery.

TRIP 6C: Mayer, Cordes, Cleator, Crown King, Bradshaw City, Palace Station, Venezia, and Maxton

Instead of returning by the same route as in trips 6 through 6b, continue back to Prescott on the historic Senator Highway, a scenic but very slow former stage route. This is **definitely not** a passenger car road, although a two-wheel drive truck can make it without much difficulty. This is an all-day, 100-mile trip. (**Note:** trying to include Oro Belle would not be advisable on this trip; you would have to rush your day too much.) Venezia has vanished almost completely, but Palace Station is a ghost town seeker's treat.

ADDITIONAL TRIPS

See chapters II, III, IV, and V, pages 31, 43, 54, and 65. All areas are within a day's return trip to Prescott.

TOPOGRAPHIC MAP INFORMATION FOR CHAPTER ONE
NEAR PRESCOTT — GHOSTS OF THE HIGHER GROUND
(For map reading assistance, consult Appendix A, page 127)

Town	Topo Map Name	Size	Importance*
Jerome	Cottonwood and	7½'	2
	Clarkdale	7½'	2
Clarkdale	Clarkdale	7½'	2
Cherry	Mingus Mountain	15'	2
Walker	Groom Creek	7½'	2
Big Bug	Poland Junction	7½'	3
Poland	Poland Junction	7½'	3
Humboldt	Humboldt	7½'	3
McCabe	Poland Junction	7½'	1
Mayer	Mayer	7½'	3
Cordes	Cleator	7½'	3
Cleator	Cleator	7½'	2
Bumble Bee	Bumble Bee	7½'	3
Crown King	Crown King	7½'	2
Bradshaw City	Crown King	7½'	2
Oro Belle	Crown King	7½'	1
Venezia	Groom Creek	7½'	3
Palace Station	Groom Creek	7½'	3
Maxton	Groom Creek	7½'	3

*1 — essential to find and/or enjoy site to the fullest
2 — helpful but not essential
3 — unnecessary for finding and enjoying site

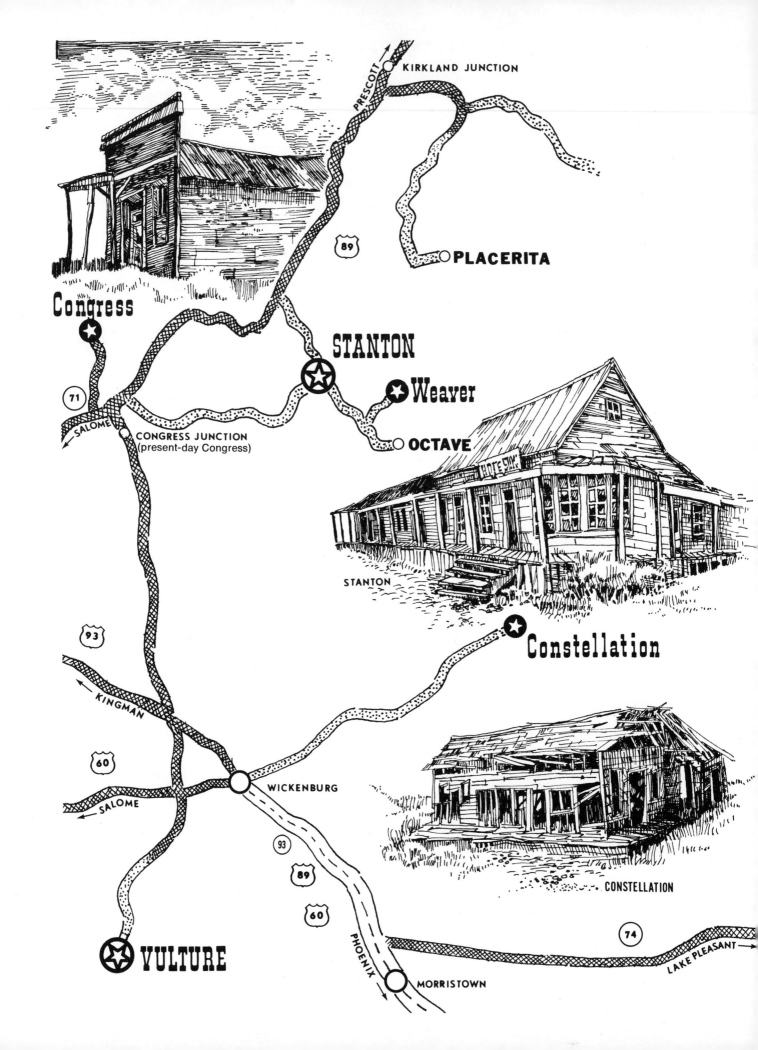

KIRKLAND JUNCTION

PRESCOTT

89

PLACERITA

Congress

STANTON

Weaver

71

OCTAVE

SALOME

CONGRESS JUNCTION
(present-day Congress)

STANTON

Constellation

93

KINGMAN

60

WICKENBURG

SALOME

CONSTELLATION

93

89

60

74

PHOENIX

VULTURE

MORRISTOWN

LAKE PLEASANT

CHAPTER TWO

THE WICKENBURG AREA

FOR MOST TOURISTS, Wickenburg (53 miles northwest of Phoenix) used to be merely a stop on the circuitous route from Phoenix to Los Angeles. Now the Interstate bypasses it. But instead of dying, Wickenburg has only lost much of the pass-through traffic and has actually gained in the long run, for now people visit Wickenburg to enjoy its shops, its excellent guest ranches, and its delightful winter climate. Ghost town enthusiasts should not miss a Wickenburg main attraction: the Vulture Mine, one of Arizona's most extensive ghosts and one of the best in the West. Stanton, Congress, and the Monte Cristo Mine, also near Wickenburg, offer buildings in good condition in rather dramatic settings. Each of the four sites is a photographer's delight.

VULTURE

Vulture is 13 miles southwest of Wickenburg on the Vulture Mine Road about 1 mile west of town.

The Vulture Mine had a considerable impact on the history of Arizona. When Henry Wickenburg discovered the strike in 1863, the northernmost Anglo settlement in the Arizona Territory was 170 miles to the south in Tucson. Wickenburg's discovery brought settlers into what is now the central part of the state and made the town of Vulture, then located on the bank of the Hassayampa River, the third largest settlement in the territory, and it nearly became the territorial capital. In order to fill the demand for feed for the livestock working at the mine, farms were developed fifty miles to the south — and the fledgling community of Phoenix was born.

Mining at the Vulture faded in the 1920s, but the mine itself didn't close until 1942. The buildings at the present site date from as early as 1877, when the entire mining and milling operation was consolidated at the mine site and the Hassayampa River townsite was abandoned. The new site was named Vulture City.

Henry Wickenburg, who gave his name to the nearby popular western resort town, died in poverty despite the riches of his find. Benjamin Phelps, who bought a four-fifths interest in the mine only three years after its discovery, never paid Wickenburg his true share. In 1905, at the age of 85, a despondent, penniless Wickenburg killed himself with a Colt revolver.

Today the Vulture Mine is a tourist attraction — an admission is charged and there are signs advertising its existence — but this is really to the ghost town enthusiast's benefit, for the town and mine have been spared much of the vandalism so common at other sites. You can still explore the buildings, well over a dozen in number and all but one under roof, at your own pace and with

Vulture. A headframe marks the location of Henry Wickenburg's original strike. In the center of the photograph are the original mill and the roof of a mine official's house; on the right is the assay office.

A close-up view of the headframe and mill at Vulture

The large assay office, constructed of rocks from the mine, is supposed to contain thousands of dollars' worth of precious metals.

relatively little company. The preservation and the extensive remains of Vulture make it the best ghost town in the middle of the state and one of the better sites in the West. Plan on two to three hours for a leisurely visit.

There are many excellent buildings, but the two-story assay office, the two schools, the mess hall, and the blacksmith's shop are particularly interesting.

Principal points of interest: On the hill: the old mill, blacksmith shop, and headframe; to the south: the newer ball mill and powerhouse; at the town: Wickenburg's home, an apartment house, bunkhouse, shops, mess hall, and assay office; to the north of the town: assorted residences, the mining superintendent's home, and the two school houses, one dating from 1877 and the other from 1936.

The school at Vulture, built in 1877. A school from the 1930s stands next door.

CONSTELLATION

To reach Constellation (the Monte Cristo Mine), turn north on El Recreo Drive (next to the Wickenburg Chamber of Commerce), which becomes Constellation Road. Follow this road northeast out of Wickenburg for 12 miles.

Constellation — probably an office or a storage building

The town of Constellation and the Monte Cristo Mine are one and the same site. The town, which was founded in the 1920s and almost totally abandoned in the 1930s, was inhabited by the miners of the Monte Cristo.

Named optimistically for the island where Edmond Dantès found the riches in Dumas's famous novel, the Monte Cristo has had several owners, and attempts to develop the presumed wealth of the mine have been undertaken periodically. Several buildings occupy the site, most still under roof and dating from the '20s. The premier building

Office or house at the Monte Cristo

Miners' quarters at the Monte Cristo in Constellation

at Constellation is the miners' quarters with its screened verandas.

Directly across from the site, on a neighboring hill to the north, is another mine building. Farther on down the road on the left is the Gold Bar Mine, which has a caretaker and is also posted against trespassers. Like the Monte Cristo, however, it is clearly visible from the road in a rather dramatic canyon. Your binoculars and telephoto lens will increase your appreciation of this mine.

CONGRESS

Congress is 16 miles north of Wickenburg and 41 miles south of Prescott on U.S. 89.

Congress is really two sites. One is the old Congress near the mine of the same name, reached by driving 2.5 miles north on Ghost Town Road just west of the intersection of U.S. 89 and Arizona 71. An adobe ruin, many foundations and pieces of tin and glass, and the Congress Cemetery are at the site. Various mine remnants and tailings are visible at the site of the Congress Mine, but all are on private property posted against trespassers.

The other site, 3 miles south of Congress, is really Congress Junction, the town that sprang up where the Santa Fe, Prescott and Phoenix Railroad came through. Still standing there are the Congress Hotel, some wooden false-front businesses, a large

A stone ruin at the site of the original Congress

A wooden false-front store at Congress Junction

The cemetery at Congress, complete with weathered markers and fence posts

adobe ruin west of the railroad tracks, and the Congress school.

The Congress Gold Mine was discovered in 1883, and by 1897 over four hundred men were employed at the mine. The biggest problem in the area was the lack of water; in fact, the only spigot in town was in front of the company store. Because of the limited water supply, fire severely damaged the town twice, in 1898 and 1900.

The mine kept the town alive until the mid-1930s. In 1938 the post office closed and was consolidated with the one at nearby Congress Junction, which had been in operation since 1906. Its name was then changed to Congress.

The cemetery at the old townsite is well worth walking through, and a telephoto lens can capture the remaining old buildings at the Congress Mine. At Congress Junction, a local resident told me about two tunnels built by Chinese who labored in the area. One connects the Congress Hotel with the adobe store across the railroad tracks, a distance of several hundred feet; the other heads from the same hotel to a small residence north of it. No one knows for certain the purpose of the tunnels.

STANTON

The turnoff to Stanton, Weaver, and Octave is 3 miles north of Congress on U.S. 89. Stanton is 6.3 miles east on a very good dirt road.

In 1863, Abraham Harlow Peeples organized a party to explore central Arizona with Pauline Weaver, a well-known western explorer, as its scout. The party camped one night at the base of a hill and shot some antelope. The next morning a Mexican was sent to retrieve a pack animal that had strayed during the night, and he returned with a handful of gold nuggets from the hill. Peeples himself is supposed to have picked up $7,000 in loose nuggets before breakfast (how could anyone have eaten anything?). The stream near where the men had camped was named Antelope Creek for the game they had shot, a second creek was named Weaver Creek in honor of the scout, and the hill was appropriately dubbed Rich Hill.

The area boomed overnight, and two communities, Antelope Station and Weaver or Weaverville, developed at the eastern and western bases of Rich Hill.

Charles P. Stanton came to Antelope Station sometime in the early 1870s. His vicious and calculating rise to power was remarkable. After being expelled from a monastery on charges of immorality while studying to be a priest, Stanton worked as an assayer at the Vulture Mine. When he moved to Antelope Station, he lived in a modest cabin near a store owned by G. H. Wilson. Wilson and the owner of the stage station, William Partridge, were not the best of friends, so Stanton decided to use this animosity to his advantage and to dispose of them both. He misled Partridge into believing that Wilson was out to kill him; as a result, Partridge murdered Wilson. For his crime, Partridge was sent to Yuma Territorial Prison, his confession written by his friend Charles Stanton. Wilson's store was taken over by his silent partner, a man named Timmerman. Timmerman was found dead shortly afterwards. In 1875, the town's name was changed to Stanton with Charles P. Stanton as postmaster. The only person remaining in town whose influence approached Stanton's was Barney Martin, who had bought Partridge's station. In 1886, the charred remains of Martin's wagon, with the bodies of Martin and his family, were found a short distance from town.

The Hotel Stanton, formerly known as Partridge's Station

Later that same year, Stanton himself was murdered by a man named Lucero in revenge for an insult to Lucero's sister. While fleeing town, Lucero met Tom Pierson, returning from Crown King. Lucero shouted, "I've just killed Stanton and I'm heading for the border." "You don't have to pull out," Pierson replied. "If you stick around, you'll get a reward."

For years, Stanton was closed to the public and a caretaker discouraged intruders. But in late 1978, the townsite was purchased by the Lost Dutchman Mining Association for use by its members and for preservation of the town. Stanton is now open for inspection and is truly worth the trip. At the town is the Hotel Stanton, the saloon, and Charles Stanton's stage stop and store, the building in which he was murdered. The structures were well preserved by their previous owner's vigilance, and the new owners insist that Stanton will not be over-restored to touristy proportions. They plan to make the Hotel Stanton habitable, however, which will require extensive renovation. The modern pay telephone attached to the beautifully weathered wood of the Hotel Stanton is not an encouraging sign. The phone notwithstanding, the hotel is a marvel of form and function: on the aesthetic side, it has a gracefully angled front corner; on the practical side, each room has a rear entrance or escape route — given Stanton's violent history, a wise architectural addition.

WEAVER

From Stanton, take the road heading southeast for 1.8 miles. A road branching to the north goes for 1 mile to the townsite.

The camp of Weaver (or Weaverville), at the eastern foot of Rich Hill, developed as a result of the gold strike made by the Peeples party (see Stanton entry, page 27). Named in honor of scout Pauline Weaver, the town enjoyed prosperity from the 1860s into the 1890s, as Rich Hill reportedly had the biggest placer deposit in the history of Arizona, yielding finds of over one million dollars.

Two buildings about one-half mile south of the main townsite and cemetery at Weaver

The Weaver post office

As the gold played out, Weaver developed a second life as a haven for Mexican desperadoes; Charles Stanton was known to have hired out some of Weaver's finest characters to do his dirty work as he rose to prominence in neighboring Antelope Station. In 1898 a newspaper account called for the elimination of Weaver because of its unsavory citizens, the most degenerate of whom was a blind old reprobate known as the "King of Weaver." Weaver received a post office in 1899, but it was moved less than a year later to Octave as Weaver's population declined.

Weaver today is a minor ghost town with a cemetery of unmarked graves, evidence of its violent past; a small, two-room rock building, which according to one source was the Weaver post office; mill foundations; a rock vault at the foot of the mill; and rock foundations and rubble in the area. About 0.5 miles south of town are two small buildings and rubble.

OCTAVE

Octave is 0.3 miles east of the turnoff to Weaver.

All that remains of Octave are several rock foundations, a large tailings pile visible from the road, and a diamond-shaped water reservoir. The site is closed to visitors by the present owner.

A placer claim was laid in the area in the 1860s by eight men who formed, appropriately, the Octave Gold Mining Company. It was not until the 1890s, however, that gold mining operations began in earnest. The post office that had been established at Weaver in 1899 was moved to Octave, along with Weaver's few remaining law-abiding citizens, in 1900. The post office remained in operation until the last day of 1942; the mine had been closed in the same year as a result of Law 208 (see page 51), but in almost fifty years of operation it yielded over $8 million in gold.

The only building at Placerita. On the hill to the west are waste dumps from short-lived mining efforts.

PLACERITA

To reach Placerita, take the dirt road heading east 0.4 miles south of Kirkland Junction, which is 22 miles south of Prescott and 35 miles north of Wickenburg. Take the right fork when the road branches after about 3.5 miles. Take another right 1.5 miles farther south. Stay on this road for approximately 5 miles until the stone house is visible on your right.

Only one stone building, mill foundations, and assorted rubble remain along Arrastre Creek at the site of Placerita (Spanish: "little placer"). The settlement featured a post office from 1896 to 1910, although Mexican miners had been working placer gold deposits as early as the 1860s.

Scattered throughout the area are various rusted 1926–1927 Model T Ford parts, most riddled with bullet holes. Unfortunately, there aren't quite enough parts to assemble and drive out.

CAPSULE SUMMARY

(In order of importance of sites)

MAJOR SITES

Vulture — one of the best ghost towns in Arizona
Stanton — three well-preserved buildings in a famous place with a violent past

SECONDARY SITES

Constellation — several buildings dating from the '20s, in good condition

Congress — two sites with buildings, a cemetery, and foundations with rubble

Weaver — several rock ruins, a cemetery, and one standing building

MINOR SITES

Placerita — one stone building and foundations

Octave — a few remains, but closed to the public

TRIP SUGGESTIONS

TRIP 1: Vulture, Congress, Stanton, Weaver, and Octave

This all-day trip from Phoenix or Prescott includes the two best sites, Vulture and Stanton, and three lesser sites on the way. About 40 miles of the trip are on very good dirt roads. If you come from Phoenix the trip will cover about 185 miles. From Prescott, the trip will be about 20 miles shorter. Plan for two hours at Vulture and an hour at Stanton and Congress.

TRIP 2: Vulture and Constellation (The Monte Cristo Mine)

The Monte Cristo Mine is 12 miles northeast of Wickenburg and has several standing buildings; you will need a truck for the occasional rough spots in the road. Plan on forty-five minutes to an hour at the site. You should allow from between seven to eight hours for the whole trip to the two sites from Phoenix or Prescott.

TRIP 3: Vulture, Salome, Harqua Hala, and Harrisburg

The Salome area ghost towns, covered in the following chapter, are 54 miles west of Wickenburg and could be included with Vulture in an all-day passenger car outing. Plan for two or three hours in the Salome area.

TRIP 4: Placerita

Placerita actually is closer to Prescott than Wickenburg by highway, but it is included in this section because its location is only a few miles north of Stanton, Weaver, and Octave as the crow flies. But one must drive all the way to Kirkland Junction, some 20 miles north of Congress, and then head south on a rather rough dirt road to reach the townsite. Placerita is a minor site and is recommended for the purist with a truck.

TOPOGRAPHIC MAP INFORMATION FOR CHAPTER TWO
THE WICKENBURG AREA
(For map reading assistance, consult Appendix A, page 127)

Town	Topo Map Name	Size	Importance*
Vulture	Vulture Mountains	15 ′	3
Constellation	Morgan Butte	7½′	3
Congress	Congress	7½′	2
Stanton	Yarnell	7½′	3
Weaver	Yarnell	7½′	2
Octave	Yarnell	7½′	2
Placerita	Peeples Valley	7½′	2

*1 — essential to find and/or enjoy site to the fullest
2 — helpful but not essential
3 — unnecessary for finding and enjoying site

Above: Headframe and ore car at Vulture

Below: The adobe and wood shops of the Vulture mine still house various implements.

The Hotel Stanton

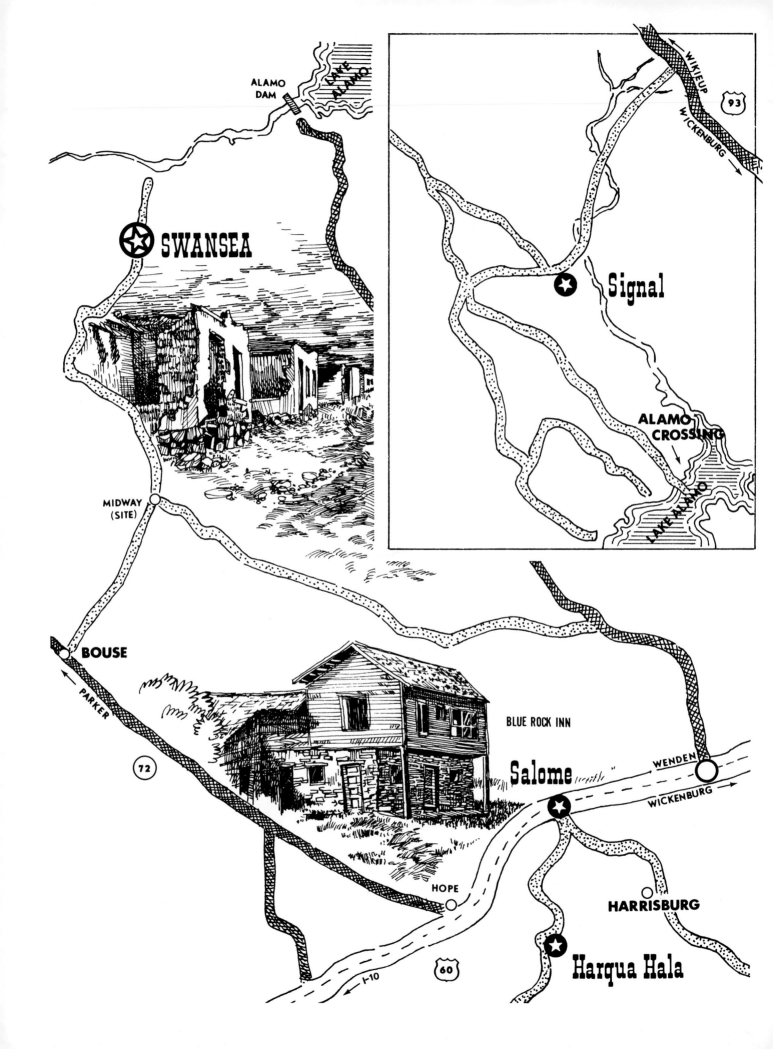

ALAMO DAM

LAKE ALAMO

⊛ SWANSEA

MIDWAY (SITE)

BOUSE

PARKER

72

WIKIEUP

WICKENBURG

93

⊛ Signal

ALAMO CROSSING

LAKE ALAMO

BLUE ROCK INN

Salome ⊛

WENDEN

WICKENBURG

HOPE

HARRISBURG

⊛ Harqua Hala

I-10

60

CHAPTER THREE

GHOSTS OF CENTRAL-WESTERN ARIZONA · THE HOT ONES

SALOME, 54 miles west of Wickenburg on U.S. 60, is the starting point for all of the ghost towns except Signal in this chapter. Between June and September, use discretion because of the intense heat. In spring, inquire locally about road conditions, as washes and rivers can make it impossible to drive to sites like Swansea and Signal.

The sites in this and the following chapter are the ghost towns that, more than any others in Arizona, demanded the heartiest settlers, for the land was stark and isolated. For the sites that are off the main roads, the same is true today, and the traveler should take extra care.

But there is something especially satisfying about visiting a remote desert ghost town. For one thing, the scenery at sites like Harqua Hala, Swansea, and Signal is of the barren beauty that only the lover of the desert can truly appreciate. Secondly, when standing at a building like the Signal saloon or the Swansea smelter, the visitor gains a genuine respect for the men and women who had the courage to live there.

SALOME

Salome is 54 miles west of Wickenburg on U.S. 60.

"Salome — Where She Danced" reads the sign on the north side of U.S. 60 in Salome. The slogan is a literary joke from Dick Wick Hall, Salome's prime mover and most famous citizen. Hall, "the Will Rogers of Arizona," wrote for the *Salome Sun* and later *The Saturday Evening Post* and was known for his tall tales and folksy humor. The town was not actually named for the biblical Salome, the dancer who received the head of John the Baptist, but rather for Grace Salome Pratt, wife of town founder Charles H. Pratt. The slogan "where she danced" came from the apocryphal tale by Dick Wick Hall that Mrs. Pratt, upon taking off her shoes during her first summer in the town, found the sand scalding hot and did an impromptu jig.

In 1904, Pratt founded the town in anticipation of the railroad. Because he miscalculated the location of the Santa Fe, Pratt had to move the town two miles to its present location, with help from Dick Wick Hall and his brother Ernest.

Salome isn't really a ghost town but rather a quiet desert community now bypassed by the Interstate. Nevertheless, it is of interest to the ghost town enthusiast because it is from here that one reaches Harrisburg and Harqua Hala. In addition, Salome has two attractions of its own — Dick Wick Hall's grave (he lived from 1877 to 1926) at the site of his home, of which only a fireplace remains; and the deteriorating two-story Blue Rock Inn, which was operated until the 1920s by Mrs. E. S. Jones and her three daughters. One advertisement in Hall's

Salome — the Blue Rock Inn

Salome Sun summarizes the Blue Rock Inn, the climate in Salome, and Hall's irrepressible humor:

> All inside rooms have Running Water on Very Short Notice and by coming at right Season of the Year you can have whichever You Prefer —

Hot or Cold (always hottest in summer). Only the Ground and Atmosphere are provided with outdoor Rooms, as no covering is Needed in the summer Season which is often quite long.

To reach Dick Wick Hall's grave, go north across the Santa Fe tracks on Center Street. The grave is at Center and Main. The Blue Rock Inn is east on Main Street toward the railroad station.

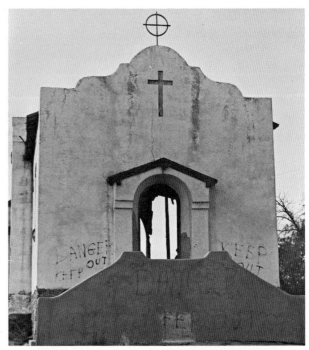

The grave of Salome's most famous resident, Dick Wick Hall

Shell of a church west of Dick Wick Hall's grave

{ 36 }

HARRISBURG

Harrisburg is 5 miles south of Salome. Take the main road that heads south from town (the Buckeye-Salome Road) past the high school. Five miles from town is a road heading off to the right where there is a concrete house on the right and mill ruins on the hill to the left. Secure permission to leave your car here and walk across the wash to the west. The monument at the cemetery is clearly visible.

Mining activity at the base of the Harquahala Mountains

Harrisburg Cemetery — the monument to slain pioneers

Captain Charles Harris, a Canadian who fought for the North during the Civil War, founded Harrisburg in 1886. With his partner, Arizona Territorial Governor Frederick A. Tritle, he erected a stamp mill to process the ore from the nearby Socorro Mine in the Harquahala Mountains. The town never reached the prominence that had been anticipated, and the post office closed in 1906.

The Harrisburg Cemetery is the reason for visiting the area. In 1849 a covered wagon party stopped at this site on the way to the California Gold Rush and was massacred by Indians. Their remains were found some months later by other gold seekers, who carried the bones to a nearby knoll and buried them. In 1936 the Arizona Highway Department erected a monument "in remembrance of the pioneers who gave their lives to the development of the West."

The memorial and cemetery are worth the visit, even though some of the graves have been unceremoniously vandalized. Scattered evidence of mining activity in the area still remains.

HARQUA HALA

Harqua Hala is 8 miles south of Salome. Take the main paved road south (the Buckeye-Salome Road) until you pass the sheriff's office (2 blocks south of U.S. 60). Take the right fork that heads due south (the other fork — the main road — heads toward Harrisburg). Other roads veer off from this one, but you will head due south for 3 miles. The road then begins a curving route past many mine ruins and tailings. When you reach a small cemetery on your right, you have reached Harqua Hala; turn to the left up to the townsite.

Harqua Hala was the site of several gold strikes; in 1762 and 1814 by Spaniards, in 1869 by a Pima Indian, and finally in 1888 by prospectors of the "modern" era. A boom town soon developed after the last strike and a post office was established in 1891, but the veins of the Golden Eagle and Bonanza claims played out in 1897. The mines, which were once sold for $1.3 million, were worked intermittently into the 1930s.

Shack at Harqua Hala

Bouse. Note the peaked false-front of this store on Plomosa Road.

Former assay office in Bouse

Old Brayton, a town constructed for tourists

The town is located in the Harquahala Mountains. In addition to the two given spellings, the name is variously spelled Hocquahala, Huacahella, Hocquehila and Har-qua-halle. The word is from the Mohave Indian "Ah-ha-qua-hale," meaning "running water" or "water there is, high up."

Because the town really had two lives, 1888–1897 (the boom years) and 1918–1932 (sporadic mining attempts), ruins of two eras exist. On the eastern edge of the site is an adobe ruin, probably a store, on the original main street. On the hill to the west is the foundation and chimney of a later home with a shored-up adobe original near it. On the western edge of the site is a building of the later years sitting dramatically on the hill. The mine and mill ruins are on the hill to the south only 100 yards or so away. Several other buildings and foundations are scattered around the townsite.

BOUSE

Bouse is 29 miles northwest of Salome on Arizona 72. From Salome, head west on U.S. 60 and turn right at Hope.

Bouse was originally called Brayton for John Brayton Martin, a storekeeper in the area. In 1907, one year after the post office had been established as Brayton, the name was changed to Bouse, probably in honor of two prominent citizens, Thomas and George Bouse.

Swansea. The base of the smelter stack is directly behind the smelter in the foreground. Company houses stand in the center of the photograph.

Now Bouse is a quiet town adjacent to the Santa Fe railroad, and the general store's principal business comes from the nearby Lincoln Ranch. One mile south of town is Old Brayton, a small tourist

Swansea's main street. Most of the buildings have been gutted by fire.

The vandalized Swansea cemetery

Saloon at Signal

Abandoned house at Signal

ghost town and museum. In addition to memorabilia from the Old West is a modest collection of Model T and Model A Fords.

On the Plomosa Road, heading north toward Swansea, are two false-front wooden buildings and a stone building that was formerly an assay office.

SWANSEA

Swansea is 24 miles northeast of Bouse. Take Plomosa Road, the only main road that crosses the tracks in Bouse, north out of town. Stay on this road for 13 miles, where you will come to the site of Midway. Here take the left fork; you will cross under a power line within 0.3 miles. Drive until there is a triangle of roads, 18.5 miles from Bouse, and take the road to the right. Within 1.5 miles you will cross over an aboveground pipeline and you will cross it again about 1 mile beyond. Swansea is approximately 7 miles from the triangle of roads.

The Clara Consolidated Gold and Copper Mining Company made Swansea its headquarters after the turn of the century. A smelter erected there enabled ore to be mined, milled, and smelted and then shipped via the Santa Fe Railroad. Prior to construction of the smelter, ores had been shipped from the area as far away as Swansea, Wales, for smelting. Byrd H. Granger in *Arizona Place Names* suggests that perhaps miners "wanted to continue shipping their ores to 'Swansea,' and so named this community." Clara Consolidated went bankrupt in 1912, but other companies worked the area until 1924.

Well over a dozen buildings remain in Swansea, although many are only adobe shells. The smelter walls are virtually intact, but the roof has partially collapsed.

Principal points of interest: adobe buildings in the center and on the eastern edge of the townsite; a cemetery (badly vandalized) just north of the easternmost adobe ruins; the smelter on the south side of the site; mine ruins; and 0.5 miles west of town, on the south side of the road, a graceful natural arch.

SIGNAL

Take the Signal road, 69 miles north of Wickenburg and 8 miles south of Wikieup

on U.S. 93. The town is 12.7 miles to the southwest. The road is excellent unless the Big Sandy River, which you must cross several times, is high. From Kingman, an alternate route is to take the Alamo Road out of Yucca off I-40.

A photograph in Jim and Barbara Sherman's book, *Ghost Towns of Arizona,* published in 1969, shows the lonely but sturdy Signal saloon. When I visited the site ten years later, the building looked just the same. Only if one frequently travels the back roads of Arizona can one truly appreciate the rarity of such an event.

In addition to the saloon, Signal features an abandoned house about 0.5 miles west and a mill foundation a few hundred yards east. On the hill above the mill is a concrete foundation for a water tank; in 1939, a man named Rebel Webb carefully signed his name in the setting cement.

Signal developed along the banks of the Big Sandy River three years after the McCracken silver mine was discovered in 1874. The town featured the usual stores and businesses and one unusual one: a brewery. The town's peak population was about eight hundred, but by the 1880s the boom was over and the town had stabilized at about three hundred. The Signal post office somehow managed to stay open until 1932.

Signal's principal shortcoming was its isolation. As reported in *Arizona Place Names,* a visitor in 1878 wrote:

Freight from San Francisco was originally brought by steamer around the California peninsula up into the mouth of the Rio Colorado, but at this time it came by rail to the west side of the river at Yuma, and thence by barge up the river to Aubrey Landing, where it was loaded on wagons and hauled by long mule teams thirty-five miles upgrade to Signal. The merchants considered it necessary to send orders six months before the expected time of delivery.

ALAMO CROSSING

Alamo Crossing was approximately 87 miles south of Kingman on the Alamo Road, and about 28 miles south of Signal.

Books and maps published as late as 1978 still show the ghost town of Alamo Crossing on the Bill Williams River. The town was a small mining community that had a post office from 1899 to 1918 and that featured one of the best-preserved stamp mills from the old days.

Alamo Crossing now sits under one hundred feet of water at Alamo Lake State Park. The Alamo Road dead-ends at the water several miles short of where the townsite used to be. A gentleman who had fished the Bill Williams River for years told me, "So that's what the name of that little town was! Well, it's out there somewhere," as he pointed to the placid blue waters. He also informed me that the lake was full of fish.

CAPSULE SUMMARY

(In order of importance of sites)

MAJOR SITES

Swansea — extensive site in a majestic setting

SECONDARY SITES

Harqua Hala — several buildings from two eras

Signal — only three ruins, but beautifully remote

Salome — only a semi-ghost; see the Blue Rock Inn

MINOR SITES

Bouse — a couple of false fronts and Old Brayton

Harrisburg — a cemetery and a monument

Alamo Crossing — submerged

TRIP SUGGESTIONS

TRIP 1: Salome, Harrisburg, and Harqua Hala

Once you reach Salome from Wickenburg, most of your driving will be over, since the other two sites are quite close to the first. A truck is suggested for Harqua Hala. The round trip distance from Wickenburg is 135 miles, from Phoenix 240 miles, and from Prescott 210 miles. You'll probably spend a total of two to three hours at the sites.

TRIP 1A: Add Vulture to trip 1 — see
Chapter Two, trip 3 (page 31).

TRIP 1B: Add Bouse and Swansea to trip 1

You'll need a truck for the trip to Swansea and about five more hours. Add 108 miles to trip 1, with 48 of them on a dirt road.

TRIP 2: Signal

Signal is 82 miles from Wickenburg, 13 of which are on a good dirt road. Signal is geographically separated from the other sites in the chapter by Alamo Lake. If your road map shows a crossing of the Bill Williams River near Alamo Lake State Park, it is out-of-date and cannot be trusted in this area.

TRIP 2A: Signal, Old Trails, Oatman, and Goldroad
See Chapter Four, trip 1a (page 54).

TRIP 3: Vulture, Salome, Harrisburg, and Bouse

For ghost town enthusiasts with a passenger car and a limited desire to travel back roads, this trip visits four sites with only 36 miles on good dirt roads out of a total of 202 miles round trip from Wickenburg.

TOPOGRAPHIC MAP INFORMATION
FOR CHAPTER THREE
GHOSTS OF CENTRAL-WESTERN ARIZONA —
THE HOT ONES
(For map reading assistance, consult Appendix A, page 127)

Town	Topo Map Name	Size	Importance*
Salome	Salome	15′	3
Harrisburg	Hope	15′	2
Harqua Hala	Hope	15′	2
Bouse	Bouse and	15′	3
	Utting	15′	3
Swansea	Swansea	15′	1
Signal	Artillery Peak	15′	2
Alamo Crossing	Artillery Peak	15′	3

*1 — essential to find and/or enjoy site to the fullest
2 — helpful but not essential
3 — unnecessary for finding and enjoying site

Above: Salome — the Blue Rock Inn

Below: Smelter at Swansea

A residence or office from the second mining era in Harqua Hala

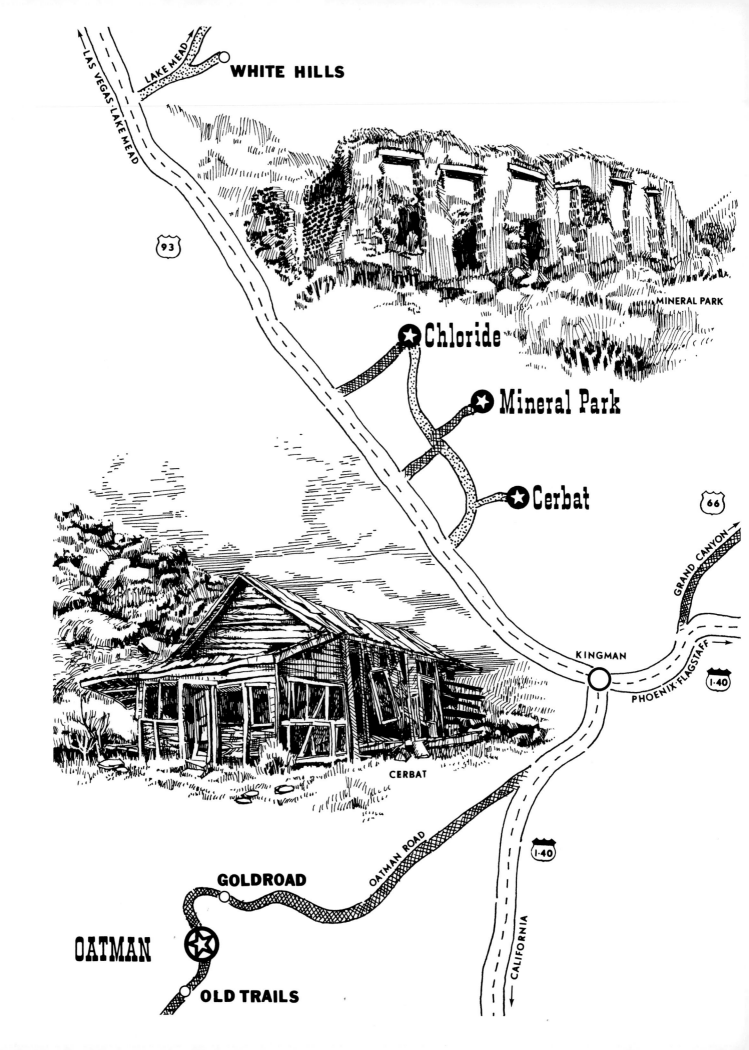

WHITE HILLS

LAKE MEAD

LAS VEGAS·LAKE MEAD

93

MINERAL PARK

Chloride

Mineral Park

Cerbat

66

GRAND CANYON

CERBAT

KINGMAN

PHOENIX·FLAGSTAFF

I·40

OATMAN ROAD

GOLDROAD

I·40

OATMAN

CALIFORNIA

OLD TRAILS

CHAPTER FOUR

MOHAVE GHOSTS

KINGMAN, 181 miles from Phoenix, 142 from Prescott, and 102 from Las Vegas, is the county seat for Mohave County and the center for ghost town trips in the area. The town was named by and for Lewis Kingman, the locating engineer for the railroad that was constructed through the area in the 1880s. The town of Kingman, like so many other railroad and Route 66 towns, is long and narrow with a string of restaurants and motels. In the center section of town, one block north of Beale Street, are several buildings you should be sure to investigate: the Mohave County Courthouse, the adjacent jail, the BPOE Hall, the public library, and many residences in the vicinity of the courthouse.

An overnight stop in Kingman is the only way to have the time to enjoy all the ghost towns in Mohave County, but an alternative trip will suggest how to see the best and still return to Phoenix or Prescott in one day. Roads to the sites are generally very good, but remember to make allowances for the tremendous heat that can hit the area from June through September. This does not mean that you should avoid the area during those months; I have visited all the sites twice in June and although it was about 100° in the afternoon, it was still enjoyable. One way to help beat the heat, of course, is to be at the first site no later than 6:00 A.M. when, even in the hottest part of the summer, the Mohave area is relatively comfortable.

GOLDROAD

Goldroad is 25 miles southwest of Kingman on old U.S. 66, and 3.3 miles north of Oatman.

The most surprising thing about the route winding up the edge of Sitgreaves Pass and over through Goldroad is that this narrow, winding ribbon of asphalt was, until 1952, the famous Route 66, the principal highway for east-west commerce and the road of hope for travelers like the Joads in *The Grapes of Wrath*. Situated on both sides of the old highway, Goldroad is now a collection of foundations and scattered roofless adobe ruins, because in 1949 the town was razed to save taxes. On the flat, western part of the townsite are the adobe ruins of what was known as Mexican Town. These comprise the major remnants of the townsite.

The Gold Road district was worked in the early 1860s, but its richest deposits were not discovered until about 1900 when a Mexican prospector named Jose Jerez, staked to $12.50 by Kingman businessman Henry Lovin, wandered into the Gold Road area and spent the night. The next morning, while searching for his burros that had strayed from camp, Jerez found a piece of quartz that showed pure gold.

A stampede to the area resulted. Lovin and Jerez sold their claim in 1901 for $50,000; the same

Goldroad — the most complete of the ruined buildings

claim was later sold for $275,000. In 1906 a French syndicate paid $500,000 for a twenty-five percent interest in the area. Lovin and Jerez's strike, which they relinquished for $50,000, was then worth forty times that. Lovin fared well nonetheless; he had a successful general store and freight company. Jerez, however, eventually drank himself into a depressed state and swallowed rat poison.

OATMAN

Oatman is 28 miles southwest of Kingman on old U.S. 66. Take I-40 south and get off at the Oatman Road-McConnico exit.

Elephant's Tooth, a huge quartz outcrop jutting up east of Oatman, was a certain sign to prospectors that great wealth lay underneath, since minerals like gold and silver often accompany quartz. The prospectors were not disappointed.

The Glory Hole Antique Shop appeared in the classic film How the West Was Won. *Note the old streetlight, its bulb still burning, on the left. Elephant's Tooth is in the background.*

Oatman — the Lee Lumber Company with its attractive variation on the standard false front

According to the legend, a half-breed Mohave Indian named Ben Taddock (Paddock by some sources) was riding along a trail, found free gold glittering in the sun, and immediately filed a claim. The Vivian Mining Company eventually purchased the claim and by 1907 had mined over three million dollars in gold from the area. The settlement was originally called Vivian, after the mine. In 1908 the Tom Reed Mine brought a second boom to the already prosperous town. It was about this time that the name was changed from Vivian to Oatman, in honor of Olive Oatman, a white girl taken captive by Indians many years before. A wealthy Mohave Indian named John Oatman, who claimed to be Olive's son, was involved in mining in the area of Vivian and might have influenced the name change, although no one knows for certain.

The story of the Oatman family's tragedy is well worth recounting even though it is not specifically connected with the town of the same name. Royse Oatman, his wife, and seven children were attacked by Apaches while they were on their way to California in 1851. The father, mother, and four of the children were murdered; twelve-year-old Lorenzo was thrown down a small cliff and left for dead, and sisters Olive and Mary Ann were captured and sold to the Mohave Indians as slaves. Mary Ann died in captivity, but apparently Olive adapted to her surroundings and even married a Mohave: there is a photograph of her with marriage tattoos. Lorenzo, who survived the massacre, organized a group to secure Olive's release from the Mohaves. Dr. Byrd Granger states that, contrary to the popular version of the story, Olive was not "rescued" at all. She knew that a party had been out looking for her for some time, and she eventually merely walked away from her "captors" to rejoin her brother. There are two versions to Olive's life story after that: one has her eventually marrying an Anglo in 1865 and dying in Texas in 1903 when in her late sixties; the other story claims she went insane after leaving her Indian family and died in an asylum only a few years after her rescue. The Oatmans who died during the initial massacre are buried in a common grave near the site of their deaths. The spot is south of the Gila River at the lower end of the bend near the town of Gila Bend.

The Tom Reed Mine, which closed in the 1930s, produced over $13 million worth of gold in almost a quarter of a century of operation. The mine's shutdown precipitated the town's decline, and during the late thirties the town survived largely as a

Cerbat — the Golden Gem mill and headframe

Miner's shack across the gulch from the Duval complex

stop along Route 66. Oatman, which once had a peak population of over ten thousand, had begun to die. The next serious blow came with the passage by Congress of Law 208, which shut down gold and silver mines in 1942 because they were not strategic materials. The mines were unable to get supplies, miners were sent to more strategic mines or drafted, and small towns dependent upon gold and silver mines dried up all across the West.

Oatman has dozens of buildings to investigate today, and its population of a few hundred is generally receptive to visitors. Be sure to see the Lee Lumber building and the old movie theater across the street; the Oatman Hotel, where Clark Gable and Carole Lombard spent the night after their marriage in Kingman; and the Glory Hole Antique Shop, which was a drugstore in the 1930s and a saloon called the Mission Inn long before that. Drive around the back streets for cabins and shacks perched at unlikely angles on hillsides, and enjoy Oatman's most pervasive residents — feral burros, which wander at will and seem to know that a camera probably means a handout.

OLDTRAILS

Oldtrails is 1 mile south of Oatman on old U.S. 66.

Founded in 1916, Oldtrails was a neighbor to the larger and older community of Oatman. The name Oldtrails was chosen because the Daughters of the American Revolution and the National Old Trails Association began a project to commemorate those routes that were used in the taming and expansion of the United States. Oldtrails was located on a route that was used by the military, including Lt. Lorenzo Sitgreaves, for whom nearby Sitgreaves Pass is named.

Only two buildings still remain at the site. One was formerly a stone assay office and has a well-preserved old gas pump standing nearby. The other structure was once a service station and motel for old U.S. 66. Both are now private residences.

CERBAT

The turnoff to Cerbat is 9 miles north of the edge of Kingman on U.S. 93. Go east on a good dirt road, turn left after 0.7 miles, turn right in 0.5 miles, and proceed 2.4 miles

down the main dirt road past a mill to the townsite.

Two wooden houses and the Golden Gem Mine's mill, all still under roof, stand at the site of Cerbat. Three tin buildings and several rock outlines of shacks stand a hundred yards or so up the road.

Cerbat, an Indian word for bighorn mountain sheep, was the name given to the mountain range north of Kingman that has supplied rich ore for well over a century. The town of Cerbat came to life in the late 1860s because of the gold and silver strikes in such mines as the Golden Gem, the Esmeralda, and the Vanderbilt. In 1871 the town was sufficiently important to be named the county seat for Mohave County, an honor it held for only two years. The post office was closed in 1912.

MINERAL PARK

The turnoff to Mineral Park is 14 miles north of Kingman on U.S. 93. The townsite is 5 miles up the paved road.

A miner from a century ago would never recognize the place. Approaching the old site, he would become suspicious because of the hum of engines and the clatter of equipment. He could look to the north and see the familiar headframe of the Keystone and, above it, of the New Moon, looking not all that much different than they did in the 1880s. But to the east, to his astonishment, he would see that the most prominent feature of the entire valley, Ithaca Peak, has disappeared. And in front of the missing mountain looms the enormous plant necessary for twentieth century mining, the giant facility of the Duval Corporation.

Mineral Park was so named in the 1870s because of the wealth found there in a park-like juniper-filled basin. The Keystone and other mines, a five-stamp mill, saloons, stores, a school, and a post office soon generated so much activity that Mineral Park became the most important settlement in Mohave County. In 1873 it wrested the title of county seat away from nearby Cerbat. Eventually the town added the refinements of the sophisticated community: lawyers, doctors, a hotel, restaurant, and a weekly newspaper. Profits increased when the railroad was sent through in the early 1880s some fourteen miles away; however, Mineral Park's citizens suffered a blow to their civic pride when, in 1887, the upstart community of Kingman, a mere railroad town, had sufficient population to claim the county seat, and a vote on the matter proved it. The officials at Mineral Park refused to accept the decision and would not give up the county records, so officials from Kingman raided Mineral Park, made off with the documents, and have held the county seat ever since. Mineral Park lost its post office in 1912 and was abandoned for many years before Duval began operations.

The adobe post office of Mineral Park still stands on the western slope of a giant tailings dump. In addition to the Keystone and New Moon headframes, a few buildings and several foundations still exist at the northern end of Mineral Park. But the best feature of the site, a small cemetery nestled beneath waste dumps and huge buildings,

The Mineral Park Cemetery, one of the
best preserved in the state

requires permission from Duval to visit. Mining engineer George Boone gave three of us a tour of the well-preserved graveyard with its variety of headstones hidden among the juniper, which is now almost an endangered species as the mine expands. I was relieved to discover that even as large an operation as Duval still has a concern for this remnant of history and is continually taking steps to safeguard the cemetery. Mr. Boone pointed out several interesting details about the cemetery and was extremely gracious to us with his time. He subsequently took us on a tour of parts of the facility and answered numerous questions about the current operation. He related some of the history associated with the site and pointed out places where Indians used to mine turquoise and where other mines used to be.

Incidentally, Mineral Park may well be a ghost town once again. Mr. Boone said that Duval estimates that their mine will be closed by about 1990.

For permission to visit the cemetery, write:
Duval Corporation
P.O. Box 3009
Kingman, AZ 86401

CHLORIDE

Chloride is 20 miles north of Kingman off U.S. 93 and 3 miles east of Grasshopper Junction on a paved road.

The first mining camp of northwestern Arizona and one of the earliest in the entire state, Chloride is now a quiet town of about three hundred people, many of whom are retirees.

The town came to life in the early 1860s with the discovery of chloride silver ore. In early times the prospectors were harassed by Hualapai Indians; in 1863, when the first strikes were made, the Hualapais killed four miners at Silver Hill camp by using guns for the first time. The Indians were eventually subdued, and by 1900, Chloride had a population of over two thousand. The town thrived into the 1940s, but the closing of the Tennessee Mine signaled the end of large-scale mining and of the prosperity of the town.

The Chloride 7½′ topographic map identifies over three dozen mines east of town. South and east of the Tennessee are Indian petroglyphs as well as murals etched by western artist Roy E. Purcell. The Schuylkill Mine, north of the Tennes-

Chloride's post office and general store

see, has a double boiler steam winch that is virtually intact.

Several buildings in town are worth inspecting, including the 1928 general store, an abandoned home on Easy Payroll Street, and the block of buildings under the "Shep's" water tower. A graveyard is west of town, just south of the main road.

WHITE HILLS

To reach the site of White Hills, take U.S. 93 north from Kingman for 44 miles and then turn right at White Hills Road. The site is 5.4 miles from the turnoff on both sides of the road. White Hills is 24 miles north of Chloride.

Only a couple of headframes, numerous waste dumps and tailings, and the rubble of one collapsed wooden building remain at White Hills.

In May of 1892, Judge Henry Shaffer located the first silver mine in the White Hills, a lesser range north of the Cerbats. He was directed there by an Indian named Hualapai Jeff, who had shown him what he had found while looking for iron oxide to be used as face paint. Only two months later, the town of White Hills had two hundred residents, a store, four saloons, and fifty tents. By 1894 the population had risen to fifteen hundred.

Water was a principal problem in White Hills. In the normal dry times it sold for one dollar per barrel, with most of the water going for the mines and the citizens taking what was left; but with heavy rains, flash floods inundated the town, washing away buildings and filling mine shafts. A flash flood on August 5, 1899, so damaged the shafts that the demise of the town began. The post office closed in 1914, but by then the town's decline had been an established fact for several years.

CAPSULE SUMMARY

(In order of importance of sites)

MAJOR SITE

Oatman — lots to see: buildings, mines, mountains, and burros

SECONDARY SITES

Mineral Park — headframes, a few buildings, and a beautiful cemetery

Chloride — small community past its glory

Cerbat — several buildings under roof; abandoned

MINOR SITES

Goldroad — deserted with extensive rubble

Old Trails — two buildings, both occupied

White Hills — mining evidence and open spaces

TRIP SUGGESTIONS

TRIP 1: (First day) **Goldroad, Oatman, and Old Trails**
(Second day) **Cerbat, Mineral Park, and Chloride**

A passenger car is quite sufficient to see all the best ghost towns in Mohave County. Trying to see them all and then return to Phoenix or Prescott in one day would hurry your visit too much. (If you cannot stay overnight, see trip 2.) The first day's distance from Phoenix is 245 miles; from Prescott, 205 miles. The second day's distance, including the return trip to Phoenix, is 230 miles; to Prescott, 190 miles.

Note: see the Mineral Park entry concerning permission to visit.

TRIP 1A: Add Signal to trip 1

Signal is 13 miles off U.S. 93, and it's worth the side trip even though it's a minor ghost town. See the Signal entry, page 41. Add 26 miles of good dirt road to trip 1.

TRIP 2: Oatman, Mineral Park, and Chloride

If time dictates eliminating an overnight stop in Kingman, then these three are the sites to concentrate upon. You should try to spend about two hours in Oatman and Mineral Park and an hour at Chloride. Total distance (and return) to Phoenix, 475 miles; to Prescott, 395 miles.

Note: See the Mineral Park entry concerning permission to visit.

ADDITIONAL SITE

Add White Hills to any of the above trips

White Hills, 24 miles from Chloride, offers little except rubble, but you may wish to visit it anyway.

TOPOGRAPHIC MAP INFORMATION
FOR CHAPTER FOUR
MOHAVE GHOSTS
(For map reading assistance, consult Appendix A, page 127)

Town	Topo Map Name	Size	Importance*
Goldroad	Oatman	7½′	3
Oatman	Oatman	7½′	2
Old Trails	Oatman	7½′	3
Cerbat	Cerbat	7½′	2
Mineral Park	Cerbat	7½′	3
Chloride	Chloride	7½′	2
White Hills	White Hills	15 ′	2

*1 — essential to find and/or enjoy site to the fullest
2 — helpful but not essential
3 — unnecessary for finding and enjoying site

Above: Deserted residence at Cerbat

Below: Mineral Park's post office

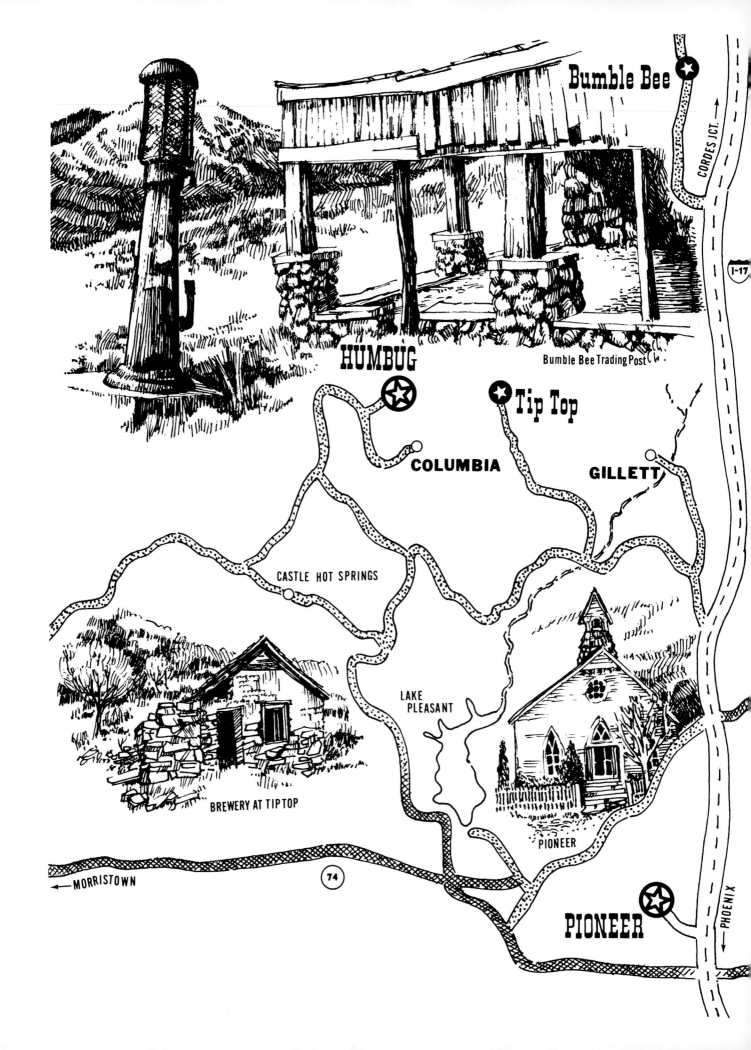

Bumble Bee

Bumble Bee Trading Post

HUMBUG

Tip Top

COLUMBIA

GILLETT

CASTLE HOT SPRINGS

LAKE PLEASANT

BREWERY AT TIP TOP

PIONEER

← MORRISTOWN

74

PIONEER

CORDES JCT.

I-17

PHOENIX

CHAPTER FIVE

NORTH OF PHOENIX

THE AREA NORTH OF PHOENIX offers something for everyone: Pioneer, a reconstructed frontier community for visitors of all ages; Humbug, a genuine, abandoned town deep in the mountains; Bumble Bee, a ghost town visible from an Interstate 17 rest stop; Columbia, a secluded spot complete with its own recluse; Gillett, a peaceful minor ghost town only one mile from the highway but far removed from civilization in feeling; and Tip Top, deep in four-wheel drive territory, waiting for the purist. **Warning:** you must cross the Agua Fria River to reach some of the sites in this chapter. At various times during the year, crossing is virtually impossible, while at other times a passenger car can make it. Inquire locally.

PIONEER ARIZONA

Pioneer is 25 miles north of Phoenix on I-17. Exit at Pioneer Road.

Pioneer Arizona is a living history museum, a 550-acre nonprofit venture into the 1870s–1890s. The largest museum of its kind west of the Mississippi, Pioneer features buildings moved from original sites from all over Arizona, as well as careful reconstructions of buildings that are based upon sketches, descriptions, and photographs. Admission is modest, and the visitor can stroll about with a brochure or take a guided horse-drawn wagon tour.

Many projects are currently under way, so one can be certain that Pioneer will be expanding and improving its already interesting attractions. Featured among the over two dozen buildings are such excellent original structures as the Sears mansion, an 1890s Phoenix Victorian; a schoolhouse and teacherage from Gordon Canyon in the Mogollon Rim high country; and several ranch buildings and cabins, including the boyhood home of Henry Ashurst, Arizona's first United States Senator. Reconstructions include many nonresidential buildings, such as an 1879 Globe church, an 1884 Phoenix bank, an 1870s Globe blacksmith shop, and an 1880s Prescott tin shop and weaving shop.

Particularly interesting to the ghost town enthusiast is the reconstruction of a miner's cabin from the Santa Rita Mountains south of Tucson, which graphically shows the primitive nature of the miner's lifestyle.

Guides dress in period costumes, and craftsmen demonstrate such pioneer activities as blacksmithing and carpentry. An opera house, which is a reconstruction of Howey Hall in Prescott, offers a melodrama for a very reasonable admission price.

Plan on spending one and a half to two hours at this delightful and educational "living museum," which is open 9–5 September through May and 9–7 June through August, seven days a week except Christmas.

Above: Pioneer's main street, complete with tumbleweeds and antique bicycles

Below: House along Boulder Creek, over halfway to Tip Top from the Agua Fria River

*Pioneer — reconstruction of the
1879 St. Paul's Methodist Church in Globe*

*The reconstruction of the original Valley National Bank
features antique tellers' windows and a massive safe.*

*Round river rocks, cut white stone, and rough blocks
make up the mosaic that was once
the Burfind Hotel in Gillett.*

GILLETT

Turn west on the Table Mesa Road overpass, 36 miles north of Phoenix on I-17. Follow the main road north for 2.5 miles. When the main road turns west, follow Mica Mule Mine Road, which continues north. In 2.5 miles you will cross the Agua Fria River. Follow the main road across the river and to the right. Turn right 0.2 miles from the Agua Fria and drive 0.2 miles farther to the townsite.

The scant remains of Gillett (also spelled Gillette) lie only one mile west of Interstate 17, but the site is protected just enough by hills and the Agua Fria River to offer a quiet retreat from nearby motorized America. Only one building is standing, the remains of the white brick and river rock Burfind

Hotel, although evidence of many rock foundations are scattered throughout the grass and brush in the vicinity.

Gillett was founded in 1878 to serve as the mill town for the Tip Top silver mine nine miles west. Named for Tip Top superintendent Dan B. Gillett, the town featured street names like California and Market, presumably in emulation of San Francisco. One of the stores in Gillett was operated by Charles T. Hayden, father of Arizona's late senator, Carl Hayden. The town itself developed a reputation for violence, with murders and lynchings beginning to occur almost simultaneously with the town's founding.

In 1886 a mill, the foundations of which are still visible today, was built at the Tip Top mine, and Gillett fell into decline. The hotel and saloon continued to serve travelers for several years, but the milling days were over. The town's post office closed in 1887 after nine years of operation.

TIP TOP

Turn west on the Table Mesa Road overpass, 36 miles north of Phoenix on I-17. Follow the main road north for 2.5 miles. Turn west at that point and continue to the Agua Fria River crossing, 3 miles beyond the turn. One-half mile after you have crossed the river, take the road heading north just before you reach Boulder Creek Ranch. About 7.5 miles up that road is Tip Top.

Have a four-wheel drive vehicle you can trust, the Black Canyon City 7½′ topographic map, and lots of time when you go to Tip Top. You will cover the 7.5 miles in about one and a half hours if you

The brewery at Tip Top

can drive all the way to the townsite. I had to walk the last 1.5 miles because of very poor road conditions. The drive is quite scenic, following the canyons of Boulder Creek, but parts of the road are rather treacherous.

The first ruin on the trip, a stone building, is 4.7 miles from Boulder Creek Ranch. At Tip Top itself are two buildings partially under roof, one roofless ruin, scattered evidence of foundations, and the tailings and foundations of the mine and mill.

The Tip Top Mine, so called because it was a "tiptop" of a prospect, was discovered in 1875. The silver was sufficiently rich and abundant that a large community of perhaps over a thousand formed along Cottonwood Creek. Ore was milled nine miles away at Gillett until 1886, when a mill was erected at Tip Top. Unlike towns such as Jerome and Bisbee, where large mining companies dominated the area, Tip Top had many small-time miners, who were referred to as "chloriders." For five years, residents had to receive mail at Gillett, but in 1880 a post office was opened at the mine site. The mine was closed in the mid-1890s after the federal government demonetized silver in 1893. The post office closed in 1895.

Important note: Some books direct you to Tip Top through Castle Hot Springs. You can't go that way. The route stops at Columbia because the owner of the Yankee Mine will not allow you to pass through. Even if you could get through, the route would be much longer and more arduous than the directions given at the beginning of this entry.

The first building at Tip Top

The main house at Humbug shows signs of recent repair and habitation.

HUMBUG

Turn west on the Cave Creek Highway turnoff 24 miles north of Phoenix on I-17. Continue 8 miles to Lake Pleasant. Humbug is 21 miles north of Lake Pleasant. Consult the Columbia 7-1/2′ topographic map.

Collapsing adobe residence at Humbug

Humbug comes into view suddenly, dramatically as you round a bend on a four-wheel drive road. About a dozen buildings, all but one under roof, are spaced out along the northern canyon above Humbug Creek. When I visited the site in May of 1979, it had been very recently abandoned, for in one building were playing cards on the kitchen table and assorted remnants of foodstuffs in the cupboards. But the droppings on the floor indicated that coyotes and rodents were the only current residents. The building left me with the eerie impression that the last tenants grew weary of cards and so decided to pack up; it all seemed so spur-of-the moment. I kept expecting someone to step out of a bedroom to ask what I was doing in his home, but the evidence that Humbug had been abandoned was indisputable.

Humbug Creek was apparently named by prospectors from the 1860s who had heard rumors of great treasure in the southern Bradshaws but had found little or nothing and so dubbed the place a "humbug." Gold placer deposits were later found in the early 1870s, however, and the communities

of Humbug and Columbia were born. In 1884 a mill, foundations of which are visible today, was constructed at Humbug along with other buildings as the community became more permanent.

The buildings surviving today probably date from about 1884, but all except one look considerably newer because they have been extensively renovated. Perhaps the town was recently used as an insular community of some sort. The main two houses could still be quite comfortable, and it is certainly possible that Humbug won't be abandoned for long. It is too attractive and desirable a place to remain uninhabited.

Columbia — foundations of the mill

COLUMBIA

Columbia is 2 miles southeast of the turnoff to Humbug. Consult the Columbia 7-1/2' topographic map.

Just downstream from Humbug are the scant remains of Columbia, an area worked at the same time as Humbug. The community once featured a mill, a post office, various stores, and a population of about one hundred, even though the Columbia-Humbug area only produced about $50,000 worth of gold.

Today one mine, The Yankee, is still being worked, and its owner is not at all receptive to vehicles on his land. One other house is above the mine, and the overlook from that property affords a view of the Columbia site. Mill foundations dating from the World War II era and a rock-walled burro corral, mine adits, and a lone stone fireplace from a much earlier time comprise the site.

A gentleman in his mid-eighties, who told me he'd "never been civilized," showed three of us around his part of Columbia. He lives in a tiny one-room trailer and routinely hikes the area to improve upon his collection of interesting rocks, pieces of glass, and occasional Indian artifacts. He informed us that there are several rattlesnakes in the vicinity that he has tamed so that they merely curl around his feet.

BUMBLE BEE

Bumble Bee is about 50 miles north of Phoenix (or 25 miles north of Pioneer). To reach the town, take the Bumble Bee turnoff on I-17 and drive 5 miles down a hilly, curving (but easily passable) dirt road. You can also reach Bumble Bee from Mayer, Cordes, and Cleator; when the road south from Cordes branches, take the left fork to Bumble Bee; the right goes to Cleator.

Hamlet's father may have been "an honest ghost," but Bumble Bee is not. The frontier street is a reconstruction of a western town that never stood at Bumble Bee nor anywhere else. The scene was created when owners of Bumble Bee had visions of a tourist mecca at the townsite. Adjacent to the picturesque but overly cute scene (a sign on a window reads "Likker") is a sturdy stone trading post/gas station. Next to it is a series of row houses, and across the street is a wood and stone schoolhouse presumably of WPA construction.

Bumble Bee was an important stage stop between Phoenix and Prescott. When a post office was established in 1879, the name was taken from nearby Bumble Bee Creek, which had been named in 1863 by prospectors who were annoyed by bumble bees in the cliffs along the creek.

The Bumble Bee Trading Post

This false-front town looks too picturesque to be genuine, and it isn't.

Row houses at Bumble Bee, the snow-covered Bradshaws in the background

Bumble Bee, visible from the Sunset Point rest stop on I-17, is now closed to the public. But all that really means is that the visitor cannot enter any of the buildings or stroll down the main street of the frontier display because of a six-foot log fence. But if you drive up next to the fence and stand on your car's hood or roof, you can get an unobstructed view. Frankly, the "town" has much more charm closed and deserted than it did open and "touristy." The school, store, and row houses are clearly in view and are the best buildings at the townsite anyway.

CAPSULE SUMMARY

(In order of importance of sites)

MAJOR SITES

Pioneer Arizona — not a ghost town, but a living museum

Humbug — recently abandoned when I was there; outstanding

SECONDARY SITES

Bumble Bee — several genuine buildings and a main street reconstruction; closed to the public but visible

Tip Top — three buildings in a remote spot; a challenge to get there

MINOR SITES

Gillett — one ruin in a pleasant spot

Columbia — only scattered evidence remains

TRIP SUGGESTIONS

TRIP 1: Pioneer, Gillett, and Bumble Bee

A passenger car can reach only three sites in this chapter: these three. Of the 120 miles traveled, only 20 will be on unpaved road. If you spend about a total of four hours at the sites, expect to be away from Phoenix for approximately seven hours.

TRIP 1A: Add Cordes, Mayer, and Humboldt to trip 1

If you want to spend a fascinating day while you travel to Prescott, consider this variation from the normal highway route. See pages 15, 14, and 12 for details on these three towns.

TRIP 2: Gillett and Tip Top

This six- to seven-hour trip from Phoenix requires a four-wheel drive vehicle. Total mileage will be about 115 miles, 72 of them on I-17.

TRIP 3: Humbug, Columbia, Tip Top, and Gillett

To visit these four towns in one day would be possible but hurried. Two friends and I had a memorable two-day getaway from civilization by seeing Humbug and Columbia on the first day, camping in Gillett, and going to Tip Top the second day. Total round trip distance from Phoenix: 160 miles. A four-wheel drive vehicle is required.

TOPOGRAPHIC MAP INFORMATION
FOR CHAPTER FIVE
NORTH OF PHOENIX
(For map reading assistance, consult Appendix A, page 127)

Town	Topo Map Name	Size	Importance*
Pioneer Arizona	Biscuit Flat	7½′	3
Gillett	Black Canyon City	7½′	2
	and New River	7½′	3
Tip Top	Black Canyon City	7½′	1
	and New River	7½′	2
Humbug	Columbia	7½′	1
	and Grosvenors Peak	7½′	2
Columbia	Columbia	7½′	1
	and Grosvenors Peak	7½′	2
Bumble Bee	Bumble Bee	7½′	3

*1 — essential to find and/or enjoy site to the fullest
2 — helpful but not essential
3 — unnecessary for finding and enjoying site

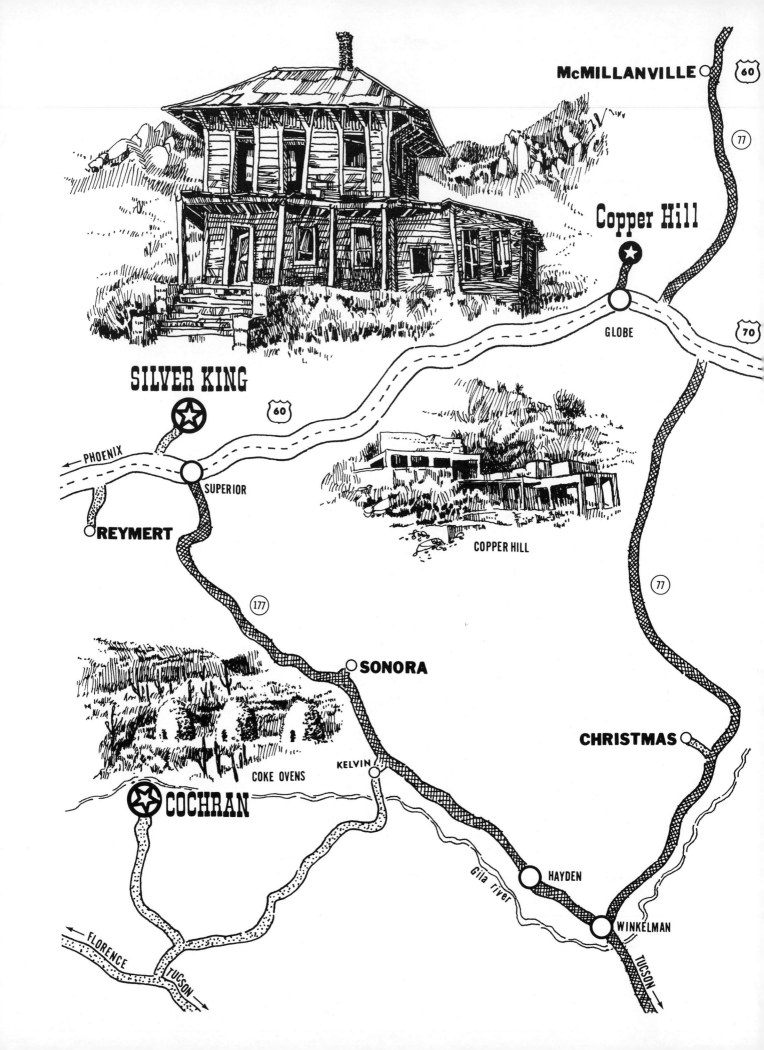

McMILLANVILLE ○ 60

77

Copstr Hill
☆

○
GLOBE 70

SILVER KING
⊛ 60

← PHOENIX

○
SUPERIOR

○ **REYMERT**

COPPER HILL

177

77

○ **SONORA**

CHRISTMAS ○

COKE OVENS

KELVIN ○

⊛ **COCHRAN**

Gila river

○ HAYDEN

← FLORENCE

TUCSON →

○ WINKELMAN

TUCSON →

CHAPTER SIX

SUPERIOR GHOSTS

THE SUPERIOR-GLOBE AREA, 63 miles east of Phoenix and 100 miles north of Tucson, features seven ghost towns. Although no one site contains a large number of standing buildings, two towns — Silver King and Cochran — have attractions so exceptional that a trip to the area is essential for any ghost town enthusiast.

In Superior itself, see the old smelter, the high school, and the hotel on the north side of the main street. Globe, 25 miles east of Superior, has many buildings from its heyday that deserve your inspection, such as the Old Dominion Hotel, the train station, and several churches.

Note: Several abandoned homes and foundations of mills are located along Arizona 177 between Winkelman and Superior. South of Winkelman beyond Dudleyville on Arizona 77 is an outstanding relic — the Feldman stage station, built in the 1870s. The adobe building with dormers in its imposing tin roof is clearly visible west of the highway. It is located on private ranch property.

SILVER KING

Silver King is north of Superior. Starting from the intersection of U.S. 60 and Arizona 177, which goes from Superior to Ray and points south, head west on U.S. 60 for about 2 miles and turn right on a road that has a sign with information about the dump. You'll know you're on the correct road when you pass a power substation on your left and can see the old smelter stack on your right. There will be a sign, "Silver King Mine — 4 miles." Follow the signs as far as your car will go. A four-wheel drive vehicle can get to the townsite if there are no locked gates; a two-wheel drive truck or car can come within 0.5 miles.

Silver King features one of the best, most photographable buildings in all of the Southwest's ghost towns — the company headquarters and guest house of the Silver King Mining Company. It's also an interesting building to explore, despite the vandalism that has taken place in the last few years and the inevitable deterioration that occurs even without the "assistance" of the thoughtless visitor. Be sure to note the little stairway heading from the second floor to the attic and the generally fine planning of this relic, probably erected in the 1880s.

The story of Silver King begins in 1872, when a soldier named Sullivan found that a mineral sample he had collected would flatten but not crush. He showed the sample to a friend, Charles Mason, but would not reveal the location of the find. Sullivan eventually left for parts unknown. Three years later, Mason and four friends were attacked by Apaches, who killed one of the men.

The Silver King Mining Company headquarters, its roof perched like an ill-fitting cap

After burying the dead man, Mason chased after a stray mule, and he found a specimen identical to Sullivan's earlier find. Mason and the other three men filed equal claims. Between 1875 and 1888, $17 million worth of silver was taken from the Silver King Mine. In 1881, Sullivan returned in bewilderment to "his discovery" to find it already thriving — he had been in California trying to raise enough money to work his find.

From 1949 to the late 1970s, the Silver King had a "queen," Grace Middleton, who with her husband tried to work the tailings for more silver. After her husband's death, she stayed on alone, guarding the premises from vandals but regaling the true history buff with affectionate stories about "her mine." In January 1979, I traveled to Silver King with two companions hoping to visit with her and gain access to the buildings. But Grace Middleton's cabin was abandoned. Magazines, shoes, sweaters, and other personal articles littered what remained of her home. Now only man's good judgment, and not Grace Middleton's tenacity, can preserve this fine old site.

Points of interest: Grace Middleton's home (the westernmost structure with its fence and flagpole),

Miner's quarters, Silver King

standing on or near the probable site of the old school; the wood frame cabin about 200 feet east; two stone miner's cabins (northeast of the Middleton home); the power plant (near the cabins); the Silver King Mining Company headquarters; the grave and headstone of King, "a true pal," a dog who died in 1940 (behind the headquarters); the mining equipment and the headframe at the mine itself (on a knoll to the southeast of the headquarters); and the Silver King cemetery, 0.5 miles northwest of Grace Middleton's house. At the intersection where you followed the sign to the right to Silver King (0.5 miles from the townsite), head northeast on the road along Silver King Wash. Proceed for 0.2 miles and park your car after you have crossed the wash twice. An old trail leads up to the right to the cemetery, which has three iron fences and one headstone. With binoculars, the cemetery is faintly visible from the back of Grace Middleton's house if you look northwest in an approximate line to the tailings on the far hills. The cemetery is not on the Superior 7½′ topographic map and is overlooked by most visitors.

REYMERT

Reymert was southwest of Superior.

To save you and your four-wheel drive vehicle an hour or two of frustration, don't bother to search for Reymert, described in two ghost town books as having fourteen or fifteen buildings. The site has been completely decimated and there are no buildings left whatsoever. Even rubble seems to have been carefully removed. Above Reymert are many mine tunnels, some of fairly recent activity, but the lone structure at the townsite is a tipped-over portable toilet with a Phoenix firm's name on it left by the crews that dismantled and removed the entire town. It is a sad sight to survey.

SONORA

To view Sonora, take the road to the scenic overlook of the Ray Mine about 8 miles north of Kelvin and 10 miles south of Superior on Arizona 177.

The only challenge with Sonora is to see it before it disappears completely as Kennecott's Ray open-pit mine engulfs it. All that was left in January of 1980 was evidence of streets, faint foundations, and utility poles. Sonora, if it exists at all when you read this book, can be viewed from the overlook at the Ray Pit by peering down at the foot of Sonora Hill, the hill to your right.

Established in 1912 by Mexican employees of the Ray Consolidated Copper Company, Sonora was named for the Mexican state that borders Arizona to the south. At one time there was a town hall occupying a four-square-block area and Spanish-style courtyards in the centers of blocks with

Sparse foundations at Sonora, overlooking the Ray Pit

buildings on the perimeters.

Although little is left to see of Sonora, you might want to view it nonetheless, as it will literally disappear in a very few years.

COCHRAN

From Florence, take the road that heads east from the prison for 16.7 miles. Turn north and follow the main road for 12.7 miles. Coming from the east, take the road from Kelvin through Riverside for 16.4 miles and then turn north. A truck is advisable for the last 12.7 miles to Cochran.

Cochran is a very special place. The townsite sits near the banks of the Gila River along the tracks of the Southern Pacific, and the mountains to the north and west are quite dramatic. Only three foundations and two sheds that were once boxcars are presently at the townsite, and the area is peaceful and remote. What makes Cochran so unusual is the presence of five spectacular coke ovens standing like sentinels up on a hill across the Gila River west of the townsite. The ovens are visible to the

The Cochran coke ovens as viewed from the south side of the Gila River. The photograph was taken with a telephoto lens.

*I used an air mattress and a watertight camera bag
to cross the Gila River to see the ovens up close.
The doorways are about 5'10" tall.*

west as you approach the town, and if the water is low you can ford the river with a four-wheel drive vehicle or cross on foot. Even if the water is too high or swift to cross, you can still enjoy the ovens from a distance. Going to Cochran early in the day affords the best photographic conditions, because the afternoon sun will create problems with glare when you try to capture the ovens with your telephoto lens.

Cochran was both a railroad stop and a mining center, with a population of about one hundred. A post office served the community from 1905 to 1915 with John S. Cochran, who named the community after himself, as postmaster.

Note: A rough jeep road on the north side of the Gila allows you to reach the ovens without crossing the river. Consult the North Butte, Mineral Mountain, Florence and Florence Southeast 7½' topographic maps. You might also check with the Pinal County Sheriff's Department regarding the condition of the road.

An oven similar to the ones at Cochran, and much easier to reach, is at Walker (see page 8).

CHRISTMAS

The turnoff to Christmas is 7 miles north of Winkelman on Arizona 77. The townsite is 1 mile west of the highway.

Several years ago, Christmas was a ghost town well

worth seeing, with a mill, several adjacent buildings, and two structures on a hill. Over the years, various parts of the mill have been destroyed, and in the spring of 1979 the mine at Christmas reopened. The result is that the site is now posted against trespassers, and tailings are encroaching upon the buildings on the hill. In a short time, Christmas will not be a ghost town site. Like nearby Sonora and Greenlee County's Metcalf (near Morenci), Christmas will either be buried or collapsed.

*Christmas — the old mill on the left
and stores in the background*

Copper was discovered in the 1880s in the Christmas area, but at the time, the land was part of the San Carlos Indian Reservation. In 1902, George B. Chittenden succeeded in having Congress pass a bill changing the boundaries of the reservation. He received news of the adjustment on Christmas Day in 1902 and left immediately to stake his claim. Over $9 million worth of copper was eventually extracted from the area. During the years of the town's post office, 1905–1935, thousands of people sent holiday cards to the town in November and December to be remailed with the Christmas postmark.

Sparse foundations and a waste dump at the site of McMillanville.
A retaining wall and remnants of shacks are closer to the creek.

McMILLANVILLE

McMillanville is 13 miles northeast of Globe on Arizona 77. On the left side of the road is a rest stop with a plaque marking the site. Either walk northwest from the rest stop to the rubble and ruins at the base of the hill, a distance of about sixty yards, or drive your car 0.1 miles north from the rest stop and take the road to the left.

McMillanville (also McMillenville, McMillen, and McMillan) lived only nine years, and all that's left today is a rock wall, the rubble of three cabins, tailings, and a mill foundation.

The area came to life when T. H. Harris and Charlie McMillan were exploring the area in 1876. The legend says that McMillan, exhausted from a night of drinking, insisted on stopping for a rest; his annoyed companion started idly picking at a ledge and found a deposit of silver.

McMillan and Harris eventually sold their claim, the Stonewall Jackson Mine, for $160,000. By 1880 a twenty-stamp mill was operating at the site and the usual saloons, shops, and boarding-houses provided for the needs of an estimated 1,500 people. That same year, the citizens decorated a Christmas tree with cigars, tobacco, dynamite fuses, grub, and bottles of whiskey — no doubt a solemn religious observance, at least for McMillanville. At the opening of the Hannibal Saloon during approximately the same year, the owner predicted a long life for the community and gallantly threw away the key to his establishment, since the doors would never need to close. In 1882 the town lost its post office. By 1885 the population of the town was one.

COPPER HILL

Copper Hill is 3 miles north of the center of Globe. Take Broad Street to Yuma Street and turn north. Turn west on High Street. About one-half block away is a road heading north with a tin building on the left-hand side. This is the road to the Copper Hill District. The road is paved for 1.7 miles, and Copper Hill is 1 mile beyond the end of the pavement on a good dirt road. WARNING: Watch for large trucks on the paved part of the road.

A tree growing on a dump is framed in the window of a roofless ruin at Copper Hill.

Several cement foundations, walls, and tailings are scattered along the road in the Copper Hill District. A roofless concrete building with steps and a lone column is on the right, and on the left farther north are the considerable remains of a gravity-feed mill perched on the side of Copper Gulch. Tailings and mine remnants dot the hills on both sides of the gulch.

Four prosperous mines north of Globe spurred the development of Copper Hill, which in the 1920s featured stores, mine headquarters, a school, a hospital, and about five hundred residents. By 1930 the town had dwindled to a few citizens; the post office closed in 1933.

The concrete remains of a mill at Copper Hill look like a Frank Lloyd Wright creation.

CAPSULE SUMMARY

(In order of importance of sites)

MAJOR SITES

Silver King — several buildings under roof, one of them exceptional

Cochran — coke ovens make this site unique in Arizona

SECONDARY SITE

Copper Hill — two major foundations and several mine remnants

MINOR SITES

McMillanville — foundations and rubble

Christmas — disappearing as mining continues

Sonora — open pit is eliminating the site

Reymert — town has disappeared

TRIP SUGGESTIONS

TRIP 1: Cochran, Sonora, and Silver King

Visit Cochran early in the day for photographic purposes and plan for two or three hours at the site if you can cross the Gila River. If not, you'll probably stay about an hour. Silver King, north of Superior, is best photographed with afternoon light, so it combines naturally with Cochran for an all-day excursion. You'll probably want to stay about two or three hours at Silver King. You will need a truck to visit both sites. The round trip from Phoenix will cover 215 miles; from Tucson, 255 miles. Sixty-six miles are on unpaved roads.

TRIP 2: Silver King, Copper Hill, and McMillanville

Copper Hill and McMillanville are minor ghost towns near Globe, and each is easily reached by passenger car. Plan for about forty-five minutes at Copper Hill and perhaps one-half hour at McMillanville. Only about 10 miles of the whole trip are unpaved, but Silver King would be reached most easily with a truck. Round trip from Phoenix is about 215 miles; from Tucson, 280 miles.

TRIP 3: Sonora, Christmas, McMillanville, and Copper Hill

This tour is for those who have passenger cars and don't want to spend much time on back roads. Only about 5 miles are unpaved, and even those 5 are very good dirt roads. The sequence of towns given is from Phoenix; if you are coming from Tucson, place Sonora last. The round trip distance from Phoenix is 250 miles; from Tucson, 270 miles.

TOPOGRAPHIC MAP INFORMATION
FOR CHAPTER SIX
SUPERIOR GHOSTS
(For map reading assistance, consult Appendix A, page 127)

Town	Topo Map Name	Size	Importance*
Silver King	Superior	7½′	2
Reymert	Picketpost Mt. and	7½′	1
	Mineral Mt.	7½′	1
Sonora	Sonora	7½′	3
Cochran	North Butte	7½′	1
Christmas	Christmas	7½′	2
McMillanville	Chrome Butte	7½′	2
Copper Hill	Globe	7½′	3

*1 — essential to find and/or enjoy site to the fullest
2 — helpful but not essential
3 — unnecessary for finding and enjoying site

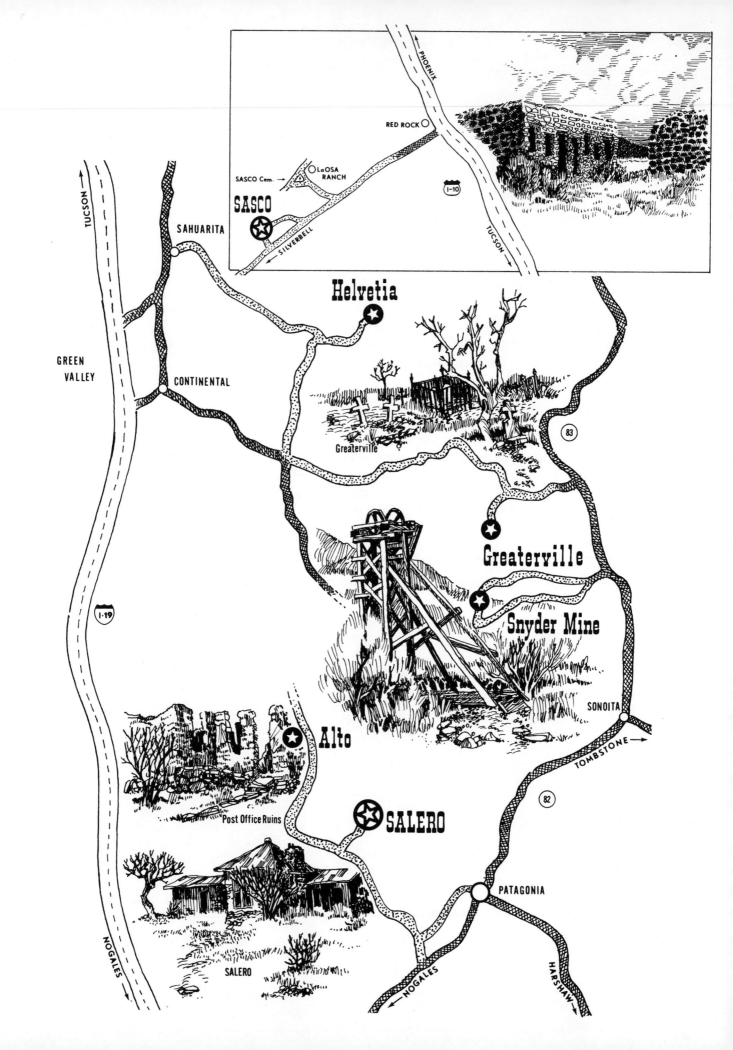

TUCSON →

RED ROCK ○

PHOENIX

SASCO Cem. → ○ La OSA RANCH

SASCO ☆

SILVERBELL

TUCSON →

I-10

TUCSON →

SAHUARITA ○

Helvetia ☆

GREEN VALLEY

CONTINENTAL ○

83

Greaterville

Greaterville ☆

I-19

☆ **Snyder Mine**

SONOITA ○

Alto ☆

Post Office Ruins

TOMBSTONE →

82

☆ **SALERO**

PATAGONIA ○

SALERO

NOGALES ↓

NOGALES ←

HARSHAW →

CHAPTER SEVEN

THE TUCSON-SANTA RITA GHOSTS

TUCSON IS SURROUNDED BY MOUNTAINS, and it was in the Santa Ritas, the range to the south, that gold and silver were discovered when the Spaniards entered the area in the 1700s. Dozens of mines but only four ghost towns remain in the rugged canyons. The towns belong together geographically, but you must approach them from different directions: Helvetia from the west, Greaterville and nearby Snyder Mine from the east, and Salero and Alto from the south.

Sasco is the one town in the chapter that is a Tucson-area site not in the Santa Ritas. It is the closest site to Tucson and can be visited in a day's outing along with selected Santa Rita ghosts.

Helvetia, Greaterville, and Alto are all minor spots. One should visit each primarily for the enjoyment of the site and its history rather than for its spare remains. Sasco and Salero are special and well worth seeing: Sasco is abandoned but intriguing; Salero is well preserved and enticing.

SASCO

Sasco is 6.7 miles southwest of Red Rock on the main road heading west from town. Red Rock is 30 miles north of Tucson on I-10.

Sasco is the best ghost town close to Tucson. Only forty-five minutes away and all but 4 miles on paved road, Sasco has two buildings, several foundations of buildings, and a smelter stack foundation. One of the challenges of Sasco is to gaze at the enormous foundations and try to picture what the whole complex must have looked like.

Sasco, an acronym for Southern Arizona Smelting Company, was a smelter town for the nearby mines at Silverbell and Picacho. The smelter was built in 1907 and closed down just after the end of World War I. The final tragic event before Sasco became a ghost town in 1919 was an influenza epidemic that killed many citizens. A small graveyard with dozens of identical concrete crosses lies northeast of the townsite as a lasting testimony to the perils of that period.

Part of the road from Red Rock is the old railroad bed of a branch line that ran daily through Sasco to Silverbell. **WARNING:** 2 miles of the road (miles 4 to 6 from Red Rock) can be quite treacherous when muddy. Do not attempt to drive the road in heavy rain or when anticipating a storm. In dry weather the road is easily traveled with a passenger car; when wet, even a four-wheel drive vehicle will have serious difficulty.

The road to the graveyard branches north to La Osa Ranch 100 yards before Sasco's most visible ruin, a roofless but substantial rock building. One source claims it was a general store, another that it was the Rockland Hotel. Directly west of this building is a two-room concrete structure with "City Hall" painted neatly above the doors. Farther west is the smelter complex, with building foundations, the stack base proclaiming "Sasco, '07," and the concrete foundations of the furnaces standing like monolithic dominoes. Be sure to notice the wall with the town's name in concrete where the railroad stopped at the smelter. A roofless adobe ruin is southwest of the smelter just off the main road as it heads to the old site of Silverbell.

Sasco — roofless rock and mortar ruins

Sasco — concrete foundations of the smelting operation

Sasco cemetery

Smelter stack base, marked "Sasco, '07"

The crumbling adobe of Helvetia's only ruin blend in with the Santa Ritas in the background.

HELVETIA

Two routes can be taken to Helvetia, one from Sahuarita and the other from Continental. I have taken both but prefer the Continental route for two reasons: the vistas of the Santa Ritas and the fact that only 8.5 miles are on unpaved roads. Take I-19 for 23 miles south from Tucson to the Continental-Madera Canyon turnoff. Follow the signs to Madera Canyon until you are 6.8 miles from Continental, where the paved road turns south to Madera Canyon. Forest Service signs will direct you immediately onto Forest Service Road 486. Follow this road to the Helvetia cemetery, some 6.6 miles away. The townsite is 1.9 miles past the cemetery. The Sahuarita, Arizona, 15′ map helps direct you to the site.

Cemetery at Helvetia

Helvetia is Tucson's most popular ghost town. As a result, not much remains at the site except a small cemetery, numerous tailings, roads crisscrossing the area, one roofless adobe ruin of several rooms, and an unusual amount of modern litter. Nonetheless, the townsite is located on the western foothills of the Santa Rita Mountains and offers in scenery what it lacks in remnants. The one adobe ruin is prominent in a photograph of the town taken in 1901. Along with that adobe building were about two dozen tents, six wooden buildings, and seven other adobe structures. Except for the one ruin, very little trace of any of them remains.

Activity in the Helvetia area began in the 1880s, and in 1891 the Helvetia Copper Company acquired claims and began mining on a large enough scale to warrant a community of a few hundred. A smelter was built in 1903, but the settlement was doomed in 1911 when the price of copper plummeted. The post office closed in 1921.

Abandoned residence at Greaterville, not visible from the road

GREATERVILLE

To reach Greaterville, take I-10 east from Tucson to the exit to Sonoita (Arizona 83). The Greaterville Road is 18 miles south of I-10. Turn right and drive 3 miles to the turnoff going to Greaterville. Turn left and take this road 1.8 miles south to the townsite.

Placer gold was found in the mile-high Greaterville area in 1874, but gold operations were hampered by the fact that water had to be packed in from Gardner Canyon a few miles south. By 1881 the gold was played out. The town became known later as a stop on "Renegades' Route," a favorite path for men trying to avoid the law when journeying between the Mexican border and Tucson.

Greaterville today is a disappointment. It is entirely on private land, and all that remains of the town are three small adobe homes, two of which are still occupied, and one collapsed wood and tin structure nearby. None is clearly visible from the public road. On a hill north of the buildings and directly east of the end of the public road is a small cemetery marked "Keep out."

The Greaterville Cemetery, on a hill north of the townsite

The headframe at the Snyder silver mine

SNYDER MINE

Turn west on Gardner Canyon Road, which is 4 miles south of the Greaterville Road and 4 miles north of Sonoita on Arizona 83. In 0.7 miles, Fish Canyon Road branches off to the north. On Fish Canyon Road, continue past the Abbey and proceed for 2.8 more miles, where you will come to a gate. On a rough but passable road not recommended for passenger cars, 3.2 miles from that gate, is Snyder Mine. The road is a Coronado National Forest road, but some of the land it crosses is private. The Mt. Wrightson, Arizona, 15′ map and the Sonoita, Arizona, 7-1/2′ map are helpful in finding the site.

The Snyder Mine was not itself a ghost town, but it is so much better preserved than other mines in the area that I have singled it out rather than including it as an attraction of Greaterville, the nearest town. The Snyder Mine was worked for silver, principally between 1894 and 1918. Joe Anderson owned the site from the 1880s until his death in the 1930s. Phil Snyder took over the mine after Anderson's death and lived in Anderson's home until he also died. When Snyder died I do not know, but I found a life insurance policy (non-drinker's, nonsmoker's) made out to him dated 1966 in a dump by the side of the road.

At the northern end of the site is the Anderson-Snyder home, a ramshackle wood-tin-adobe creation, and the charred remnants of a garage burned by vandals in 1978. Farther south on the road is a tin building from the 1930s and the headframe and adits of the mine itself. The road is public, but the buildings are on private property and "no trespassing" signs are clearly posted. When two friends and I established with the caretaker that I was only taking pictures and had neither firearms nor destructive intentions, I was allowed limited but cautiously friendly access to the site. The caretaker is understandably outraged at the senseless vandalism that has taken place at the mine.

The road continues past the mine and becomes a real four-wheel drive challenge that after approximately four beautiful but punishing miles joins back up with Gardner Canyon Road. Returning the way you came is faster and much easier on your vehicle.

The former home of Joe Anderson and Phil Snyder. A pin-up girl hanging on a wall is the only current resident.

Salero, looking much the same today as it did in the 1880s. See the historical photograph in Jim and Barbara Sherman's Ghost Towns of Arizona, *page 133, for a comparison.*

A hundred-year-old adobe building at Salero

SALERO

The Salero Road is about 2.5 miles southwest of Patagonia. Turn north and ford Sonoita Creek. (The hardest part of the trip is the fording of this creek. If it is running normally, a passenger car can make it across with some caution. If it is too high, go into Patagonia and inquire about the road through the bird sanctuary, which avoids the crossing.) Salero is approximately 7.9 miles from the creek crossing.

Salero is a beautifully preserved ghost town, considering that it is virtually unrestored. More than likely it has never been totally abandoned. A picture of the town taken in 1909 shows the same adobe buildings that are still under roof today, although some of the tin roofs are new.

According to a long-standing account but without documented evidence, Mexicans worked the Salero Mine in the 1700s under the direction of Jesuits. The mine's name, "saltcellar" in Spanish, supposedly was bestowed because a saltcellar was fashioned from the silver of the mine to decorate the dinner table of a visiting bishop.

John Wrightson and Gilbert Hopkins, two Americans who were a part of the Salero Mining Company that worked the mine starting in 1857, are important to us today because their names grace two of the highest peaks in the area, Mt. Wrightson and Mt. Hopkins. Both men were killed by Apaches in the 1860s.

The buildings now at the site probably date from the time of Salero's post office, 1884–1890, when the mine was active under the direction of George Clark.

On the west end of the site are two residences, one of which is still occupied. One large adobe house is up the street to the east, and across from it is a many-roomed building with a spacious courtyard. To the west is a rock structure down near a stream.

The road is posted against trespassers, and the owner does not welcome visitors, according to the security guard of the nearby Salero Ranch. But there is a road immediately south of the town that is the property of the Salero Ranch, not the Salero Mine, and I was given permission to photograph the town from the ranch property.

The home of Salero's lone resident

The Alto post office

ALTO

From Salero, continue north to the Salero Ranch. Drive north from that spot 2.2 miles, following the sign to Josephine Canyon. Note the mine tailings on the mountains to the east.

All that is left of Alto (or Alto Camp) is a roofless adobe post office built in 1907. Nonetheless, the ruin is located in a beautiful high desert setting that offers the photographer or artist truly creative possibilities.

Gold discoveries were made in the Alto area as early as 1687, but modern-era mining did not begin until 1875 when the Gold Tree Mine caused the establishment of the community known as El Plomo. "Plomo" means "heavy" in Spanish and refers to the lead deposits found in the area. The date when the name of the camp was changed to Alto (Spanish: "high") is unknown. The post office, which served a community of several hundred, was discontinued in 1933.

CAPSULE SUMMARY

(In order of importance of sites)

MAJOR SITES

Salero — beautifully preserved from the 1880s, but on private property

Sasco — extensive foundations

SECONDARY SITE

Snyder Mine — two buildings under roof, headframe, and mine remnants; all on private property

MINOR SITES

Alto — a post office ruin in a beautiful location

Helvetia — one adobe ruin, extensive mining evidence, and a small cemetery

Greaterville — three standing buildings (two occupied) and a cemetery

TRIP SUGGESTIONS

TRIP 1: Sasco

Planning on about three hours for this 77-mile round trip from Tucson will allow you one and a half hours at the site. Only about 6 miles of your trip will be on unpaved road, but beware of treacherous muddy spots in rainy weather.

TRIP 2: Salero and Alto

This six-hour round trip from Tucson through either Nogales or Sonoita will cover just under 200 miles, about 25 of which are unpaved. Consider making this a loop trip down through Sonoita and Patagonia and back through Nogales.

TRIP 3: Helvetia

Helvetia is only 39 miles from Tucson. Plan for about three hours for the round trip. The last 8 miles to Helvetia are unpaved.

TRIP 3A: add Greaterville to trip 3

Where Forest Service Road 486 heads for Helvetia, the main dirt road goes to Arizona 83. Greaterville is about 12 miles away on that dirt road. Return to Tucson via Arizona 83.

TRIP 3B: Sasco, Helvetia, and Greaterville

Combine trips 1 and 3 or 3a together.

TRIP 4: Greaterville, Snyder Mine, Salero, and Alto

Go to Greaterville via the Sonoita route. Snyder Mine requires a truck or four-wheel drive vehicle. Go through Sonoita and Patagonia to reach Salero and Alto. Plan on at least nine hours.

Note: You could see the two best sites of the area — Sasco and Salero — on the same day, but that would require a great deal of Interstate driving and backtracking. You would enjoy each much more by going on two separate trips.

TOPOGRAPHIC MAP INFORMATION
FOR CHAPTER SEVEN
THE TUCSON-SANTA RITA GHOSTS
(For map reading assistance, consult Appendix A, page 127)

Town	Topo Map Name	Size	Importance*
Sasco	Red Rock	15 '	2
Helvetia	Sahuarita	15 '	2
Greaterville	Sahuarita and	15 '	3
	Empire Mts.	15 '	3
Snyder Mine	Mt. Wrightson and	15 '	1
	Sonoita	7½'	1
Salero	Mt. Wrightson	15 '	2
Alto	Mt. Wrightson	15 '	2

*1 — essential to find and/or enjoy site to the fullest
2 — helpful but not essential
3 — unnecessary for finding and enjoying site

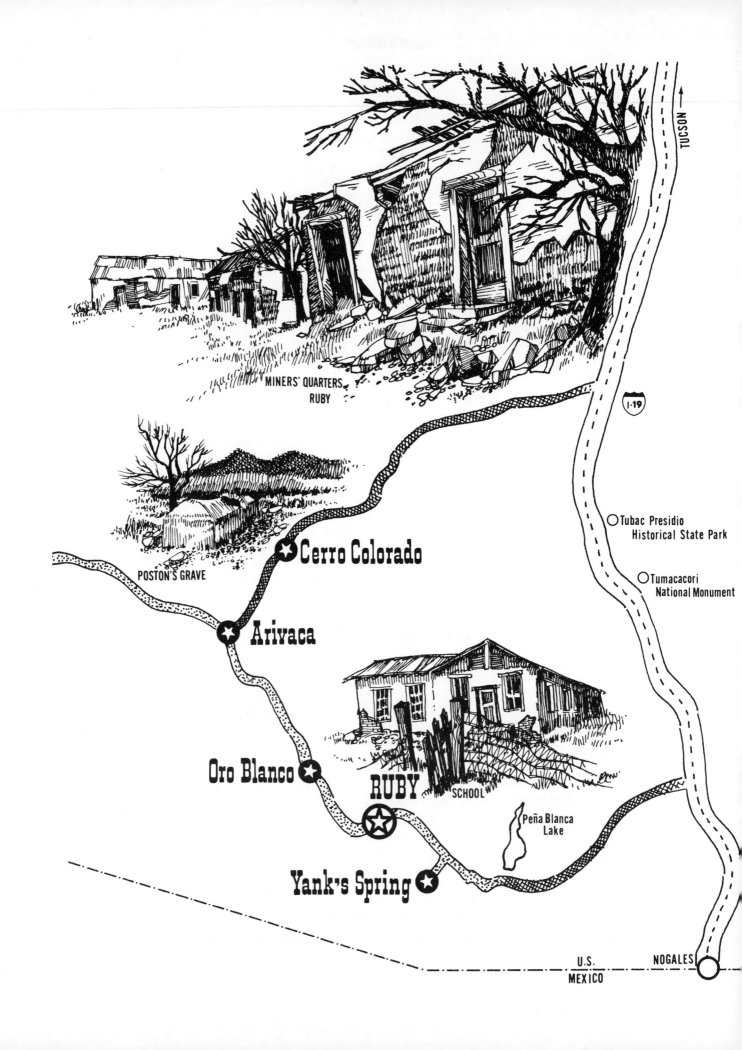

MINERS' QUARTERS
RUBY

POSTON'S GRAVE

★ Cerro Colorado

TUCSON

I-19

○ Tubac Presidio
Historical State Park

○ Tumacacori
National Monument

✪ Arivaca

Oro Blanco ✪

RUBY ✪ SCHOOL

Peña Blanca
Lake

Yank's Spring ✪

U.S.
MEXICO

NOGALES

CHAPTER EIGHT

THE RUBY LOOP

FOUR GHOST TOWNS and three spots of historic note are the attractions of this area south of Tucson. You'll visit Cerro Colorado, site of gold mining from the 1850s; Arivaca, a semi-ghost with some inviting old buildings; Oro Blanco, a stage stop dating from the 1870s; Ruby, the most extensive ghost town in southern Arizona (closed to the public but partially visible from the road); Yank's Spring, a ruin in scenic Sycamore Canyon; and, on the return trip on I-19, Tumacacori Mission and Tubac Presidio Historical State Park, which are important historic spots but not ghost towns and therefore not included in this book.

CERRO COLORADO

Cerro Colorado is 56 miles south of Tucson. Take I-19 to the Arivaca exit and head west. At Arivaca Junction on the old Nogales Highway, turn to the right and then to the left following the sign to Arivaca. Cerro Colorado is 15 miles from this point on the right side of the road. There are two or three roads leading in; the first and best is at the mailbox of the Circle 46 Ranch. Up the road about 0.2 miles on the left is the Poston grave.

Cerro Colorado effectively reflects the occasional violence and strife between Anglos, Mexicans, and Indians. Prior to the Gadsden Purchase in 1853, the area had been worked by both Spaniards and Mexicans. Two years after the area became part of United States territory, the Sonora Exploring and Mining Company, headed by Charles Poston, acquired the property. Their operation went relatively successfully until just before the Civil War, when mishaps in the mine caused mistrust between the Mexicans and Indians working the mines and their Anglo employers. Many miners left, some claiming the mine to be haunted. During the Civil War, Apaches began frequent raids on the mine because troops had been removed from the area for more strategic duty. To compound the problems, John Poston, left in charge of the mine workings by his brother Charles, executed his foreman for stealing bullion. As a result, Mexican miners stole as much as they could and headed back to their homes in Sonora with a tale about a $70,000 buried cache. Mexican outlaws then crossed the border to retrieve it and killed John Poston and two of his employees. The cache was never found, if indeed it ever existed.

The site features scant adobe foundations and crumbling walls from the early days and cement foundations from later efforts, including mill remnants. What makes Cerro Colorado significant is the grave of the murdered John Poston, up on the hill behind the mill foundations.

John Poston's grave at Cerro Colorado

Ruins of the early mining efforts at Cerro Colorado

ARIVACA

Arivaca is 9 miles west of Cerro Colorado, 24 miles west of I-19.

Arivaca, a peaceful ranching community and only a semi-ghost, has several buildings well worth seeing. The town was originally the site of a Pima Indian village. The Mexican occupation of the area began with a land grant given to Thomas and Ignacio Ortiz in 1833. They built a ranch on the grant, La Aribac, but by the time the land became part of the United States after the Gadsden Purchase, the ranch was deserted. Charles Poston bought the ranch land from the Ortiz family in 1856 for $10,000 in gold when he began his Cerro Colorado operations. Mining has long since ended, but cattle ranching continues in the area.

On the right as you enter the town from the east is a general store still open for business. Across the street is a former army barracks with twelve foot ceilings, which is now a private residence. Farther down the street on the left is a large adobe ruin where Theresa Celeya's brothers supposedly came to hide after they robbed the Vulture Mine near Wickenburg. They were rumored to have buried their loot of two gold bricks at Theresa's house, but, of course, no trace has ever been found. But it isn't for lack of trying: the back yard is pockmarked with old mounds and craters.

Take the street just west of the general store heading north. On the left is the area of the mili-

Grave in the Arivaca Cemetery

tary installation, the cemetery (where Theresa Celeya was buried when she died in 1937 at the age of 102), and an unusual old fire hydrant made by the Eddy Valve Co. Off to the right is a school featuring a beautiful bell.

Arivaca. Rumors of buried treasure have robbed this rambling adobe of a peaceful abandonment.

Stage stop/residence at Oro Blanco

ORO BLANCO

Oro Blanco is 9 miles south of Arivaca.

The original Oro Blanco, which existed through the 1880s and '90s, was south of Ruby. This site south of Arivaca, sometimes referred to as New Oro Blanco, was originally a stage stop, and the main adobe building, still in very good condition, was built as a stage depot in about 1877, according to the caretaker. Later, a doctor made the stage stop into his home. Behind the residence are several outbuildings, including an old assay office that was later a Chinese cook's quarters.

To the south of the buildings are relics from the era such as a wagon frame and other equipment. South of the site and across the wash, visible from the buildings, is a small cemetery. Contact the caretaker before you explore the area. He can also show you interesting memorabilia in a shed on the property.

RUBY

Ruby is 4 miles south of Oro Blanco and 13 miles south of Arivaca; or, coming the other way, about 30 miles northwest of Nogales on Arizona 289, the Ruby Road, off Interstate 19.

The town of Ruby is a magnificent obsession to the ghost town enthusiast. Only Jerome and Vulture, far to the north, are in its class as far as extensive remains are concerned, so Ruby is definitely the most desirable site in southern Arizona. Almost three dozen buildings are under roof, and the spot constitutes a photographer's dream. But Ruby is effectively sealed off to the curious, and one can only gaze from the road at a small portion of the buildings because of a locked gate, dogs, and the obstructing hills.

Although the mine had been worked as early as the 1870s, the town did not receive its permanent

The Oro Blanco cemetery, across the wash south of the stage stop

Ruby, from the gate: if you do not have permission to enter, this is about all you can see with binoculars or a telephoto lens. Montana Peak is in the background.

Ruby — the mine superintendent's home

Not much is left of Hank and Yank's ranching effort — the sign is as large as the ruin.

name until two months after Arizona received statehood in 1912. Postmaster and storekeeper Julius Andrews named the town in honor of his wife, Lillie Ruby. A new owner purchased Andrews's store and built a second one on a new site to replace the original in 1913. His choice of site was supposed to have been unlucky, since some believed the store to have been built over a padre's grave. Indeed, ill fortune did plague the store, which is still standing, as it was the site of two brutal robbery-murders in 1914 and 1921. In each case, two people tending the store were killed.

In 1927 the Eagle Picher Company purchased the claims and Ruby expanded to a peak population of 2,000, but the company closed down the mine and town in 1941. Today, a Dallas firm mines the site, and visitors are forbidden because of chemicals that are stored in the town for use in further mining operations.

I was fortunate enough to visit Ruby in February, 1978, with a group led by Jim and Barbara Sherman, authors of the excellent source book, *Ghost Towns of Arizona*. All groups and individuals are now being turned away, however. Perhaps at some future date the town will be reopened to selected visitors.

From the road you can see a mine office (the highest building on the southern slope), headframe, mill ruins, and three or four residences. Bring binoculars and a telephoto lens.

If you can secure permission to enter the town, you will be busy: on the northern hill, you will see the store, jail, residences, school, and the school's three-door outhouse (boys, girls, teachers); in the lake area, visit residences and a cement vault, which was probably used for chemical storage; when you go up to the southern slope, investigate the mine headquarters, shops, mill ruins, headframe and mine shaft; and finally, on the western slope, examine mine officials' residences and miners' quarters.

YANK'S SPRING

Yank's Spring is 5 miles east of Ruby heading toward Peña Blanca Lake. Take Forest Service Road 218 to Sycamore Canyon, 0.3 miles south of the main road. When you are coming from I-19, the site is 18.3 miles west on the Ruby Road.

Yank's Spring (also called Hank and Yank Spring) consists of a small adobe ruin, the remains of an unsuccessful ranching effort in the 1880s by "Yank" Bartlett and Hank Hewitt. Yank and Hank were teamsters who hauled freight for the military in southern Arizona. In 1886 the ranch was attacked by Indians, and Yank's son Johnny escaped and went to Oro Blanco for help. The returning force routed the Indians, who had already killed a neighbor and wounded Yank.

The ranch site is at the entrance of Sycamore Canyon, a beautiful and peaceful hiking area.

CAPSULE SUMMARY

(In order of importance of sites)

MAJOR SITE

Ruby — easily the best ghost town in southern Arizona, although closed to the public

SECONDARY SITES

Oro Blanco — one historic building and cemetery

Arivaca — several good buildings and one ruin

MINOR SITES

Cerro Colorado — interesting principally for Poston's grave and mine and mill remnants

Yank's Spring — beautiful spot with real history but only a minor ruin

TRIP SUGGESTIONS

TRIP 1: Cerro Colorado, Arivaca, Oro Blanco, Ruby, and Yank's Spring

An all-day trip out of Tucson, the Ruby Loop covers about 160 miles, 90 of which are on Interstate 19. I have made the loop in a passenger car, but I felt much better about the route when on a return visit I had a truck. Local weather conditions can affect the road since you must cross several normally dry washes or trickling streams that can become impassable during the rainy season.

Plan to spend one hour in Cerro Colorado, forty-five minutes in Arivaca, one and a half hours in Ruby (or ten minutes at the gate if you do not have permission to enter), and one-half hour at Yank's Spring.

TRIP 2: Cerro Colorado, Arivaca, Oro Blanco, and Ruby

If you have a passenger car, you can avoid the roughest part of the loop by returning from Ruby back through Arivaca.

TOPOGRAPHIC MAP INFORMATION
FOR CHAPTER EIGHT
THE RUBY LOOP
(For map reading assistance, consult Appendix A, page 127)

Town	Topo Map Name	Size	Importance*
Cerro Colorado	Arivaca	15'	2
Arivaca	Arivaca	15'	3
Oro Blanco	Oro Blanco	15'	3
Ruby	Ruby	15'	3
Yank's Spring	Ruby	15'	2

*1 — essential to find and/or enjoy site to the fullest
2 — helpful but not essential
3 — unnecessary for finding and enjoying site

Above: The Ruby school last saw pupils at the beginning of World War II.

Below: The slide at the Ruby school

Above: Miners' quarters at Ruby

Below: Store at Ruby, the scene of two violent robberies

TUCSON

TOMBSTONE

SONOITA

83

82

SUNNYSIDE
TOWNSITE

FT. HUACHUCA

NOGALES

CANELO

PATAGONIA

HARSHAW

SUNNYSIDE

MOWRY

PARKER
CANYON
LAKE

NOGALES

Washington Camp

Duquesne

DUQUESNE
SCHOOL

Lochiel

SUNNYSIDE SCHOOL

CHAPTER NINE

SOUTH OF SONOITA

I N NO OTHER AREA in southern Arizona can one find so many sites really worth exploring in so beautiful and peaceful a setting as in the area south of Sonoita and Patagonia.

Sunnyside is unique in the West — a ghost town that was a religious community, a town without a violent past; Mowry features many remains from as far back as the Civil War; Duquesne has several wooden structures still in habitable condition; and Harshaw features one of the most attractive buildings in Arizona. And a passenger car can visit them all.

SUNNYSIDE

To reach Sunnyside, take Arizona 83 south from Sonoita, following signs to Parker Canyon Lake, 26 miles from Sonoita. (An abandoned school is in Canelo on the right hand side of the road, 16 miles out of Sonoita.) Continue past the lake going south for about 2 more miles to a turnoff on the left marking the way. Follow the road for 3 miles directly into the townsite.

Sunnyside is singularly fascinating for four reasons: its origins, its well-preserved state, its peaceful solitude, and its caretakers. Check in with Mr. John McIntyre and his wife, who live in a home immediately adjoining the open square that contains the

four main buildings of Sunnyside. Mr. McIntyre, now in his late eighties, can tell you remarkably interesting details about the history of Sunnyside. He speaks from personal experience, since he was raised in this small community and attended, at around the turn of the century, the very schoolhouse that stands in the northeast corner of the townsite.

Sunnyside is unique because, in contrast to the normal violence and vice of most frontier mining towns, it was founded by a man of true Christian spirit, Samuel Donnelly, who created Sunnyside as a religious commune with mining as the foundation for the economy and brotherhood as the foundation for the lifestyle.

Sunnyside came into existence in 1898 when Donnelly moved his followers, called Donnellites by outsiders but who thought of themselves simply as "good Christians," down to the site near the Lone Star Mine. Many families had separate quarters, but all families ate together in a communal building. Chores were divided according to talents, and the community boasted such refinements as skilled craftsmen and music teachers. The followers of Brother Donnelly were generous with their earnings, contributing money and goods to needy passersby and even giving scholarships to students at the University of Arizona in Tucson.

Samuel Donnelly died in 1901, but the community continued for many years. By 1932, however,

The Langford house at Sunnyside. The well still supplies some of Sunnyside's water.

John McIntyre captivates my University of Arizona ghost town class with anecdotes about Sunnyside as it was in the early 1900s.

Brother Samuel Donnelly's modest home

Sunnyside's children attended class in the Langford house until this school was erected at around the turn of the century.

the mine had been closed and the town was sold to a private owner.

Principal points of interest: the schoolhouse (northeast corner of the meadow), the Gattrell house (southwest corner), Brother Donnelly's cabin (the smallest and least pretentious structure), the Langford house (northwest corner), the sawmill and corral (across the stream to the west), and Mr. and Mrs. McIntyre's personal collection of memorabilia.

Reminder: You will be a guest on private property. Please treat it with the respect that this beautiful and peaceful place deserves.

HARSHAW

Harshaw is 9 miles south of Patagonia on a good dirt road. To reach Patagonia from Tucson, take I-10 east, then turn south on Arizona 83 to Sonoita, 26 miles away. Turn right at the intersection of highways 83 and 82 and continue 12 miles to Patagonia. In Patagonia, turn left in front of the old depot and left again at the first street. Take this paved road heading uphill and out of town past the church. Continue 9 miles to Harshaw and turn left at the townsite sign. You are now on Harshaw's former main street.

Harshaw — an adobe residence

Harshaw was named for David Tecumseh Harshaw, a cattleman and successful miner. The Hermosa Mine, opened in 1877, was the foundation for the town's economy. The peak population of Harshaw was supposed to have reached 2,000. At that time the main street ran for three-quarters of a mile.

On that main street today are two cabins, one beautiful wood and brick building with a gracefully sloping tin roof covering a porch, several outbuildings, and an occupied home whose owner raises peacocks. The cemetery is across the wash and up a small hill to the west of the road coming from Patagonia. It has many headstones and wrought-iron work that date from the 1880s. Farther down the road toward Mowry is an adobe ruin on the left-hand side.

Harshaw's principal building: note the artistic brickwork of the chimney, the graceful tin porch roof, and the handsome wood columns.

Mine company headquarters at Mowry

MOWRY

Mowry is 5 miles south of Harshaw or approximately 14 miles south of Patagonia. At the sign marking the townsite, turn left and proceed until you see adobe ruins to your right and left.

Mowry is one of the "must see" ghost towns in southern Arizona for several reasons: it is a true, abandoned ghost; it sits in a beautiful, peaceful location; it has extensive adobe and stone ruins (none under roof); and it has an interesting history.

Sylvester Mowry owned and worked the lead and silver mine formerly called The Patagonia from the years 1859–1862, but in 1862 he was abruptly arrested and charged with being a Confederate sympathizer, a crime that cost him several months' imprisonment at the infamous Yuma Territorial Prison and the seizure of his property. He was eventually released for lack of evidence, and he went to England hoping to raise enough of a stake to reopen operations at Mowry; however, he died in England at the age of thirty-nine. The mine, under new owners, prospered through the turn of the century, and the town featured a post office until 1913.

Occasional evidence of the plaster exterior still clings to the adobe at Mowry

Spend time walking the area — there are foundations, tailings, a collapsed shaft to the north of the townsite, a windowless stone building adjacent to the hole, and about half a dozen adobe ruins. A small cemetery is "located on a knoll not far from town," according to one source, but it is not on the topographic map of the area and I was unable to locate it. May you have better luck.

Mowry. This windowless rock structure with the cupola on the roof stands near the collapsed shaft.

WASHINGTON CAMP
AND DUQUESNE

Washington Camp is 5 miles south of Mowry; Duquesne is 1 mile from Washington Camp. Note: the road to Duquesne can get rather rough and may require a truck.

In the 1890s, Duquesne and Washington Camp bloomed together when the Duquesne Mining and Reduction Company founded Duquesne (where the mine, company headquarters, and residences for mine officials were located) and contributed to the boom of Washington Camp (which developed bunkhouses, a general store, a school, and miners' residences). The post office for the area moved from one town to the other from 1880 until it was closed in 1920.

The road from Harshaw and Mowry goes through the middle of Washington Camp, and you may be disappointed at the dearth of ghost town atmosphere — some of the original buildings have been "modernized." Leaving the town to the south, the road forks to the right to Duquesne or straight ahead to Lochiel. Before you drive to Duquesne, take the main road south about 0.2 miles where the road crosses a wash. Up to your left are the

Duquesne's largest building, probably the mining company headquarters

ruins of the Duquesne School. Be sure to see the board nailed between two trees many decades ago, which forms a pleasant seat.

Residence on Duquesne's main street

Now either return to the fork in the road and take the shorter, more rugged road to Duquesne or continue down the main road for 1 mile to a turnoff to the right; this road is the other end of the Duquesne loop road but is quite a bit smoother.

Duquesne contains many well-preserved wood buildings and residences, including a stately home, partly obscured by trees and shrubs but easily recognizable by its large screened porch. All the buildings are marked with "no trespassing" signs, but they are close enough to the road to afford photographs and judicious inspection.

LOCHIEL

Lochiel is 3 miles south of Duquesne.

Lochiel is included here because it is mentioned in some ghost town books. It is a charming border town, called La Noria by Mexican-Americans, with a cemetery on the hill behind the church. Several buildings, most in use, date from an earlier era, but as a ghost town Lochiel is a bit disappointing.

Fray Marcos de Niza, the first European to enter what is now the United States, crossed at what is now Lochiel in April of 1539. A monument marks that historic moment.

CAPSULE SUMMARY

(In order of importance of sites)

MAJOR SITES

Sunnyside — five buildings under roof, beautiful location — a "must"

Mowry— half a dozen adobe ruins; very scenic

Harshaw — one graceful building and a picturesque hillside cemetery

SECONDARY SITES

Duquesne — several well-preserved buildings in excellent condition

Washington Camp — ruins of a school, some mine ruins

Lochiel — interesting cemetery, historic monument, peaceful border town

TRIP SUGGESTIONS

TRIP 1: Sunnyside, Lochiel, Duquesne, Washington Camp, Mowry, and Harshaw

All of the sites in this chapter can be visited in one all-day trip from Tucson. The total distance is about 175 miles with 65 miles on good unpaved roads. The order of towns can be reversed if you desire, but I'd see Sunnyside early in the morning: it will brighten your whole day.

TRIP 2: Harshaw, Mowry, Washington Camp, Duquesne, and Lochiel

Seeing Sunnyside on another trip, such as Trip 3 below, would permit you a more leisurely pace at these sites south of Patagonia. Total distance from Tucson is 160 miles, 45 of which are on unpaved roads.

TRIP 3: Sunnyside, Fairbank, Tombstone, Gleeson, Courtland, Pearce, and Cochise

See Trip 1, Chapter Ten, page 117.

TOPOGRAPHIC MAP INFORMATION FOR CHAPTER NINE SOUTH OF SONOITA
(For map reading assistance, consult Appendix A, page 127)

Town	Topo Map Name	Size	Importance*
Sunnyside	Huachuca Peak	7½′	3
Harshaw	Harshaw	7½′	2
Mowry	Harshaw	7½′	2
Washington Camp	Harshaw	7½′	3
Duquesne	Duquesne	7½′	2
Lochiel	Lochiel	7½′	3

*1 — essential to find and/or enjoy site to the fullest
2 — helpful but not essential
3 — unnecessary for finding and enjoying site

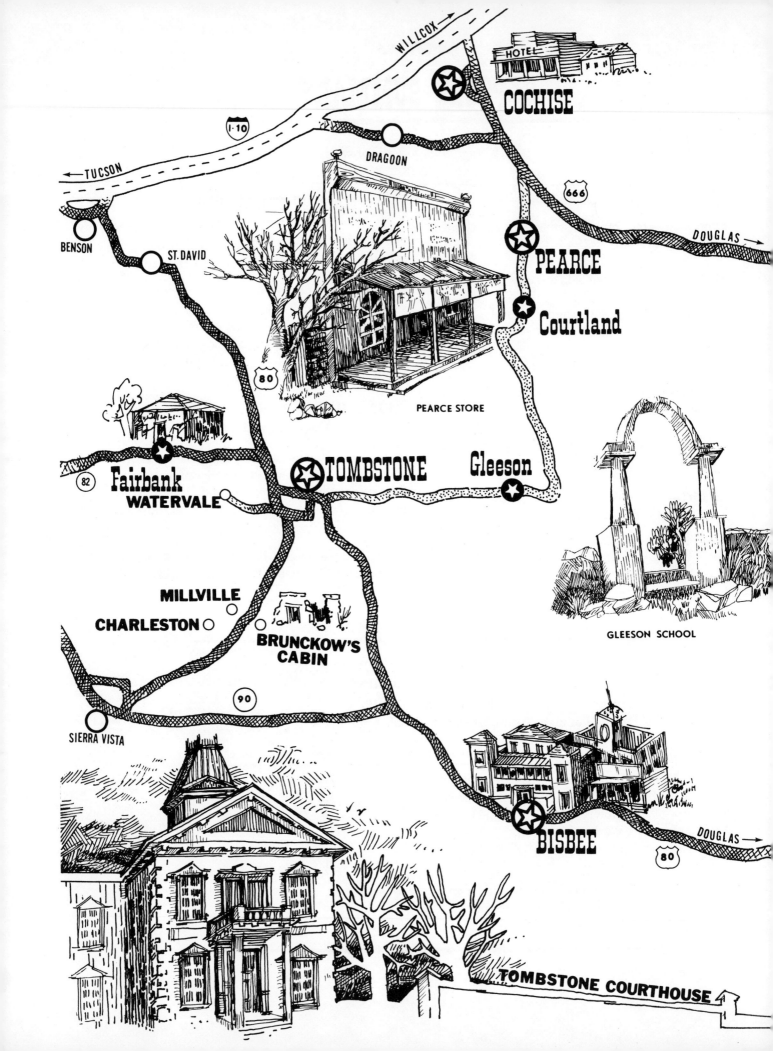

HOTEL

COCHISE

WILLCOX

TUCSON

I-10

DRAGOON

666

DOUGLAS →

BENSON

ST. DAVID

PEARCE

Courtland

80

PEARCE STORE

82

Fairbank

WATERVALE

TOMBSTONE

Gleeson

GLEESON SCHOOL

MILLVILLE

CHARLESTON

BRUNCKOW'S
CABIN

90

SIERRA VISTA

BISBEE

DOUGLAS →

80

TOMBSTONE COURTHOUSE

CHAPTER TEN

TOMBSTONE TERRITORY

IT'S ALMOST AS IF Tombstone Territory had been created for ghost town exploring. On all roads leading from Tombstone are sites worth investigating. The attractions have remarkable variety, such as Tombstone, bustling and famous; Watervale, deserted and ignored; Brunckow's Cabin, important yet overlooked; and Bisbee, picturesque and inviting. In the Territory are good restaurants, crafts shops, tours, antique stores, and special accommodations at the Copper Queen and the Cochise Hotel. Yet the visitor can still find solitude at spots like Pearce, Courtland, and Gleeson, and find a relaxed, comfortable pace in Cochise and Bisbee.

TOMBSTONE

Tombstone is 69 miles southeast of Tucson. Take I-10 east to Benson and then U.S. 80 south to Tombstone.

"The Town Too Tough to Die" is perhaps the most famous town of the Old West, but it is not a ghost. Some excellent buildings from the 1880s make a visit very worthwhile, but one must sift through a number of rather touristy spots to see the genuine historic attractions.

In 1877, Ed Schieffelin left Camp Huachuca to prospect the promising hills some thirty miles to the northeast in Apache country. He was warned that all he would find there would be his tombstone, so when he made his first real strike, he called the mine The Tombstone. Schieffelin found the silver that began the rush, but businessman John B. Allen was the driving force behind the town itself. It is Allen Street today that is the main thoroughfare of historic and tourist appeal, featuring such famous places as the Bird Cage Theatre, the Crystal Palace, and the O.K. Corral Office and Stable. On Fremont Street, one block north, are the City Hall, Schieffelin Hall, and the battle site of the gunfight at the O.K. Corral. One block south of Allen is Toughnut Street (after the mine of the same name, a "tough nut to crack"), which features the beautiful 1882 Tombstone Territorial Courthouse and Fire House Engine Company #1. Also in Tombstone are such attractions as the Rose Tree Inn Museum, Fly's Photo Gallery, the Wyatt Earp Museum, the Wells Fargo Museum, and legendary Boot Hill. Most of the attractions charge an admission.

After touring Tombstone, take Allen Street west of town to the Schieffelin Monument, the spot where Ed Schieffelin said he spent two beautiful nights before his silver strike, camping near water and hiding from Apaches. Now he is buried there, at his specific request.

Principal points of interest: Do not miss St. Paul's Episcopal Church (Third and Safford Streets) and

Tombstone's City Hall

Tombstone's courthouse, the center of county government until the town lost the county seat to Bisbee

*St. Paul's Episcopal Church, one of Tombstone's
most often overlooked buildings*

the Tombstone Territorial Courthouse State Historical Monument and Museum. Drive or walk the back streets of the town for period structures. Choose from among the myriad tourist attractions those that seem the most enjoyable to you.

FAIRBANK

Fairbank is 10 miles northwest of Tombstone on Arizona 82.

Fairbank was not a mining town; founded in 1882, it was the railroad supply depot and stage terminus for mines in the area, so it was an important place to busy communities like Tombstone, Patagonia, Nogales, and Charleston. A hotel, a dining room, saloons, and assorted stores catered to the railroad and stage traffic.

Jeff Milton, one of Arizona's most authentic western heroes, thwarted a robbery attempt by the notorious Stiles-Alvord Gang at Fairbank in 1900. Milton was inside the express car guarding the Wells Fargo box and its payroll when the gang

The Fairbank Commercial Company

rushed the train as it stopped at Fairbank. Milton was hit by early gunfire and threw the key to the payroll box out the opposite door so that the gang couldn't open the box. The robbery was aborted as townspeople gathered. At least two of the gang were also injured, and Milton's arm was permanently disabled from his wound.

Today, Fairbank has several buildings worth seeing, but the area has posted "no trespassing" signs and some of the buildings are partially hidden by brush. But the Fairbank Commercial store, which was open for business and contained the post office into the mid-1970s, is easily visible from the highway and the railroad overpass. Near the store is a public telephone, so I did not hesitate to cross the cattleguard with the "no trespassing" sign on it to "check the phone number of a friend in Tombstone." There are also two houses immediately adjoining the store to the north. On the south side of the highway is a wood and tin building. West of the store along the railroad tracks is a residence clearly of railroad company origin. What was once a beautiful railroad station, a quarter of a mile down the tracks, has been torn down. Nevertheless, one can stand on the highway bridge over the tracks and look down to the spot where the famous lawman Jeff Milton was shot while doing his duty.

Rock ruin at Watervale, across the wash from the well. The cone in the distance, left, is the Schieffelin Monument.

WATERVALE

Drive west on Allen Street past the Tombstone Cemetery (not Boot Hill). You will see a wash ahead and a road veering off to the right at a 45° angle with a windmill ahead. Take that dirt road to the ruins.

Watervale actually predates Tombstone by a few months and served as the water source for the larger community for many years. There is some disagreement as to whether the stone building, mill ruins, and spring at this location are actually those of Watervale. According to *Arizona Place Names,* the townsite was three miles north of Tombstone at the base of Tank Hill; Jim and Barbara Sherman, in

Brunckow's Cabin

Ghost Towns of Arizona, say it was south of town near the Lucky Cuss Mine. But W. J. Way's booklet *Ghosts and Ghost Towns — Southeastern Arizona* claims that this site is actually Watervale. Whichever location is correct, this is the only site with a surviving ruin. Whether it is Watervale or not, it is picturesque and worth visiting on the way to the Schieffelin Monument.

BRUNCKOW'S CABIN

Brunckow's Cabin is 7.2 miles southwest of Tombstone on the Charleston Road. At that point you will see a turnoff to the left just before a cattleguard. Across the wash and clearly visible on a knoll is the "cabin," actually an adobe ruin.

Brunckow's Cabin is one of those sites for the purist who wants a feeling for history while he stands on a certain spot. The cabin is a dramatic contrast to the activity in nearby Tombstone.

Frederick Brunckow was a German scientist and engineer who immigrated to the United States and who had begun a mine near this cabin by 1858, over twenty years before Ed Schieffelin found the vein that made Tombstone a Western legend. Mexicans raided Brunckow's mine, however, killed him, and threw his body down the shaft.

After Brunckow's death, the deserted cabin, because of its view of the surrounding area, was used as a rendezvous for many notorious outlaws. Scene of double-crosses, ambushes, and raids, the building became known as "the bloodiest cabin in Arizona's history." Ed Schieffelin himself, on his way to discovering the silver riches only seven miles away, stayed in the cabin in the late 1870s.

Today, one room with a corner fireplace remains, and the adobe outlines of the remainder of the cabin are deteriorating into the surrounding hillside. Hundreds of cars pass daily en route between Tombstone and Sierra Vista, their occupants oblivious to the proximity of the cabin with the bloody past.

CHARLESTON AND MILLVILLE

Charleston and Millville are located on the banks of the San Pedro River 9 miles southwest of Tombstone. Charleston is on the west bank; Millville is on the east, 100 yards from the river.

About 2 miles beyond Brunckow's Cabin are the sites of Charleston and Millville, two deserted ghost towns that were the mill towns for the Tombstone mines. When the mines were flooded late in 1886, these two towns began to die.

Many of Charleston's remains were destroyed during World War II when soldiers from Ft. Huachuca used the area for war games. Only a few crumbling adobe walls remain. At Millville are some larger ruins, including foundations of the mill on the side of the hill.

Warning: The land surrounding both sites is fenced off and "no trespassing" signs are prominently displayed. With binoculars or a telephoto lens, you can see some of the Millville ruins. The sites are not worth challenging the authority of the signs, however, which announce that intruders will be prosecuted.

GLEESON

Gleeson is 15 miles east of Tombstone on a road that begins on the east end of Tombstone on Fremont Street. A highway sign directs you to the turn.

The site of earlier turquoise deposits worked by Indians, Gleeson was named for John Gleeson, a prospector from nearby Pearce. The town thrived on its copper from the Shannon Mine from about 1909 through World War I; however, by 1939 Gleeson had declined, and in that year the town lost its post office. The last mine closed in 1953.

Today, Gleeson's principal attractions include the following: the cemetery on the north side of the road entering the town; the bar (still open) on what was the main street; two buildings north of the bar; the 1909 jail directly across the street to the south of the tavern; the school foundation and the graceful arch at the entrance to the school; and the adobe hospital ruins on the east end of town on the north side of the road.

North of town on the main street are the adobe remains of the Musso home. The Mussos were prominent mine owners in the community and their home was the finest in Gleeson. The best

Gleeson hospital, with the mines of Gleeson in the background

The Musso home, once Gleeson's showplace residence

Although the Gleeson school was dismantled to provide timbers for the mines, the remarkable arch remains.

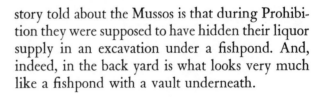

story told about the Mussos is that during Prohibition they were supposed to have hidden their liquor supply in an excavation under a fishpond. And, indeed, in the back yard is what looks very much like a fishpond with a vault underneath.

COURTLAND

Courtland is northeast of Gleeson on a good dirt road. One mile out of Gleeson, turn left and go almost 3 miles, where you will see a fork in the road going off to the east; just 0.4 miles north of that fork, on your left, is an old stone building; two others are across the road to your right. One-half mile farther

The Gleeson jail

The Courtland jail, virtually identical to Gleeson's

When the light is right you can still pick out some very faint letters painted across the top of this Courtland store.

up the road, which curves to the east, is the jail on a hill to your right.

Courtland is a ghost town in the true sense, since it is apparently abandoned. The lone buildings are the jail (virtually identical to the one in Gleeson, 5 miles away), and three buildings 1 mile south of the jail.

Courtland's boom began in 1909 with hundreds of miners working for four separate mining companies. The town proceeded through prosperity to decline; by 1942, when the post office was closed, the town's fate was clear, and many buildings were sold and taken to other locations. In the last decade alone, two brick stores have disappeared. Their foundations are visible on the west side of the road out of Courtland heading toward Pearce.

Warning: There are many open mine shafts in the area.

PEARCE

Pearce is 9 miles north of Courtland, and 29 miles northeast of Tombstone. Coming from the other direction, it is 22 miles south of I-10 on U.S. 666, exit 331.

Pearce was the last of the Arizona gold rush camps. Jimmie Pearce, a Tombstone miner, found gold in 1894 and staked a claim, which became the Commonwealth Mine. A post office was established two years later, and the population reached almost fifteen hundred. The Commonwealth closed in the Thirties, and, in the normal pattern of such towns, the population dropped drastically.

The principal attraction is the Pearce Old Store, which contains hundreds of items of antiquity, many of them for sale. In addition to the Old Store, be sure to see the many abandoned homes; the post office building (directly across the street from the

Pearce's Old Store, built in 1893, is a marvelous amalgam of adobe, stucco, wood, and ornamental tin.

Pearce's Old Store

Abandoned residences in Pearce

Old Store); the remnants of the Commonwealth Mine and Mill (east of the post office on the side of the hill); the Pearce Church, dedicated in 1914 (southwest of the Old Store); and the cemetery (west of town on the road north of the Old Store).

COCHISE

Cochise is 78 miles east of Tucson off I-10 on U.S. 666, and 16 miles north of Pearce.

Cochise is not a ghost town, but it has two such outstanding buildings at the intersection of its main streets that the ghost town enthusiast should not pass it up. The town sits at what was the junction of the Southern Pacific and the long-defunct Arizona Eastern railroads. The trains carried the ore and supplies from the nearby mining towns of Pearce and Johnson.

The picturesque old Cochise Country Store, the hub of activity in the town, is open for business. As fine a building as it is, it is second in town to the marvelous Cochise Hotel across the street. Built in 1882, the hotel still accommodates guests and

serves meals (both strictly by reservation only). It is decorated with period furniture, and each room is its own delightful museum. The food is excellent. In addition to the guest rooms are the old Wells Fargo office with its Greene Cattle Company safe, a comfortable parlor with a sofa reputed to have been Jenny Lind's, the charming dining room, and the kitchen with its beautiful icebox. Behind the hotel is a gift shop housed in an old harness shop. Quite simply, the Cochise Hotel is one of the most interesting buildings in the West.

Nearby points of interest: Cochise Stronghold, 20 miles south of Cochise, where the legendary Apache chief is buried somewhere among the rocks; the Amerind Foundation Museum, 15 miles southwest of Cochise at Dragoon (advance arrangements required); and near Dragoon, the historic Dragoon Springs Butterfield Stage Station, built in 1858. (Take the dirt road heading west and then south from Dragoon to the turnoff to Jordan Canyon, 2.3 miles from Dragoon. Turn left and proceed for 1.1 miles. The stage stop ruins and four graves are inside a fenced-off area to your left.)

Cochise's Country Store, a classic western commercial building

*The Cochise Hotel was built for the railroads,
so the front faces the tracks.*

*The parlor of the
Cochise Hotel*

Bisbee's mining museum, formerly the Phelps Dodge headquarters

BISBEE

Bisbee is 94 miles southeast of Tucson and 22 miles south of Tombstone on U.S. 80.

Scattered throughout Tombstone Canyon, Bisbee's buildings are nestled under rock cliffs, hanging on hillsides, and propped over streams. The narrow streets and winding steps invite the visitor to walk rather than drive while exploring this enchanting town. Although it is not as spectacularly dramatic as northern Arizona's Jerome, Bisbee surpasses Jerome in charm. It is a "must see" town.

An Indian scout named Jack Dunn discovered ore in Mule Pass in 1877. He and his partner George Warren developed the Copper Queen Mine, a name chosen because the men hoped that the claim would approach the success of the then prosperous Silver King Mine in Pinal County (see page 67). In 1880 the two men were joined in the area by a rival mining interest, the fledgling Phelps Dodge and Company, who purchased property near the Copper

Queen. To avoid costly litigation that could only delay the development of both claims, the two companies merged as the Copper Queen Consolidated Mining Company. The town itself was named for a shareholder in the company, Judge DeWitt Bisbee, who in fact never visited the site. Mining operations were carried out on a large scale for an astounding ninety years, from 1885 to 1975. By contrast, the Silver King Mine, whose success Dunn and Warren wanted to emulate, had a mere thirteen years of peak mine life!

Like Jerome, Bisbee today is a semi-ghost. When Phelps Dodge finally shut down operations in 1975, many people felt that Bisbee was doomed to wither, but concerned townspeople and an influx of talented young craftsmen have brought Bisbee to what might be called a state of careful balance; it is neither too touristy, too quaint, nor too dilapidated; it is simply being carefully preserved.

Just prior to entering Bisbee's business district, stop at the small turnout on the north side of the

Bisbee — the commodities exchange building in famous Brewery Gulch.
Be sure to look in the windows at the enormous blackboard.

Bisbee — the Pythian Castle

road for an unobstructed view of most of the town. Acquaint yourself with some of the major landmarks — the Copper Queen Hotel, the Pythian Castle, the IOOF Hall, and other buildings of interest — because when you are actually in the town you may need them for points of reference, since the one-way, dead-end, and twisting streets can be confusing as you try to find the road that will take you to that elusive house on the hill. But that is part of the fun of Bisbee.

Across U.S. 80 from the central business district is the entrance to the tour of the underground mine, which closed in 1975. The tours are conducted from 10 A.M. to 5 P.M.

Southeast of Bisbee, on the way to the neighboring towns of Lowell and Warren, is the awesome Lavender Pit, the open pit mine that closed in 1974. An observer staring at this remarkable hole might think that the name came from some miner with a touch of the poet in him who noticed the distinctly purplish tinge the pit gets toward dusk. But no such luck — it was named for a vice-president of Phelps Dodge.

Principal points of interest: The Mining Museum, the buildings of Brewery Gulch, Pythian Castle, the Copper Queen Hotel (reservations are advised), the mine tour, the Lavender Pit, and countless houses, businesses, municipal buildings, and winding streets.

CAPSULE SUMMARY

(In order of importance of sites)

MAJOR SITES

Bisbee — beautiful semi-ghost; a photographer's delight

Tombstone — historic but touristy; choose attractions wisely

Pearce — The Old Store is exceptional

Cochise — The Cochise Hotel is unique

SECONDARY SITES

Gleeson — several buildings; an interesting site

Fairbank — one very good building

Courtland — three good buildings

MINOR SITES

Brunckow's Cabin — one ruin rich in lore

Watervale — one ruin

Millville and Charleston — private property, no trespassing

TRIP SUGGESTIONS

TRIP 1: Sunnyside, Fairbank, Tombstone, Gleeson, Courtland, Pearce, and Cochise

This all-day trip from Tucson (leave early, arrive late) covers about 245 miles with 85 miles unpaved. See page 95 for details on Sunnyside. After leaving Sunnyside, go through Elgin to reach Fairbank (consult a highway map). At the sites, you might estimate: Sunnyside, one and a half to two hours; Fairbank, fifteen minutes; Tombstone, one and a half to three hours; Gleeson, one hour; Courtland, thirty minutes, and about one hour each for Pearce and Cochise.

TRIP 2: Tombstone and Bisbee

The two most extensive towns in the area are Tombstone and Bisbee. This 190 mile round trip will take all day because of the number of spots of interest at each site. You might wish to stay at the historic Copper Queen Hotel in Bisbee (reservations are advisable).

TRIP 3: Fairbank, Tombstone, Watervale, Brunckow's Cabin, and Millville

Except for Tombstone, this trip features pure, minor ghosts. You will see only ruins at the sites, but each offers something special. Millville can only be viewed from a distance. Plan about eight hours for the whole trip. Approximate distance is 172 miles from Tucson, with all but 4 miles on paved roads.

TOPOGRAPHIC MAP INFORMATION
FOR CHAPTER TEN
TOMBSTONE TERRITORY
(For map reading assistance, consult Appendix A, page 127)

Town	Topo Map Name	Size	Importance*
Tombstone	Tombstone	7½'	2
Fairbank	Fairbank	7½'	3
Watervale	Tombstone	7½'	2
Brunckow's Cabin	Fairbank	7½'	2
Charleston	Fairbank	7½'	1
Millville	Fairbank	7½'	1
Gleeson	Outlaw Mountain	7½'	3
Courtland	Pearce	15'	2
Pearce	Pearce	15'	3
Cochise	Cochise	15'	3
Bisbee	Bisbee	7½'	2

*1 — essential to find and/or enjoy site to the fullest
2 — helpful but not essential
3 — unnecessary for finding and enjoying site

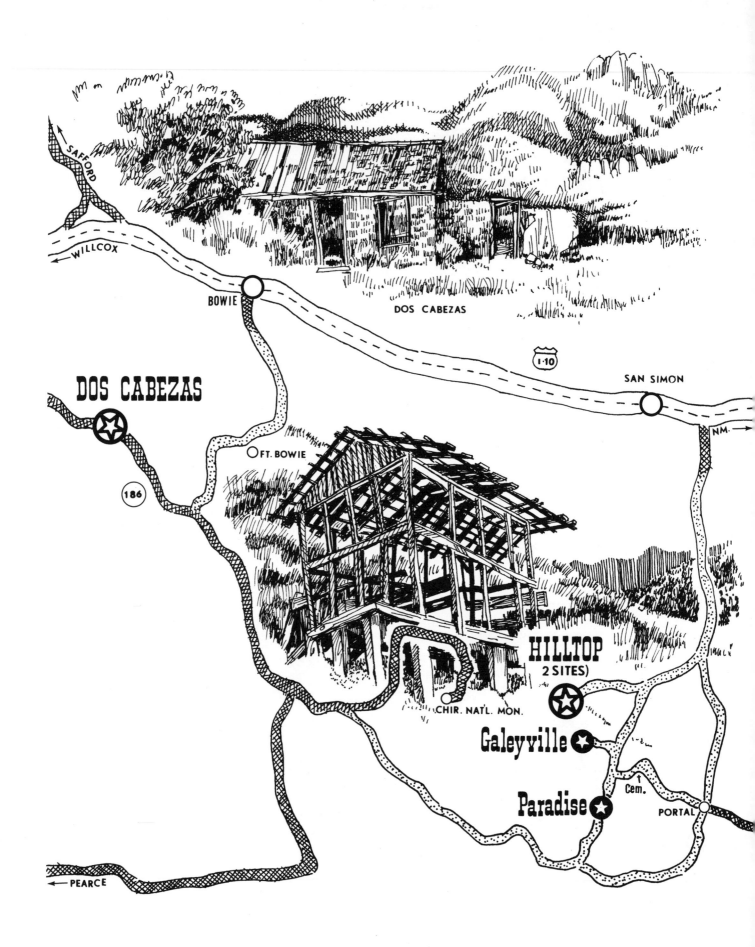

SAFFORD

WILLCOX

BOWIE

DOS CABEZAS

I-10

SAN SIMON

NM.

DOS CABEZAS

186

FT. BOWIE

HILLTOP
2 SITES)

CHIR. NAT'L. MON.

Galeyville

Paradise

Cem.

PORTAL

PEARCE

CHAPTER ELEVEN

THE CHIRICAHUA GHOSTS

TRAVELERS NEW TO THE CHIRICAHUAS are usually surprised at the scenery. Only forty miles from the plains of Willcox, the Chiricahuas offer forested mountains, abundant wildlife, and spectacular changes of the seasons.

The ghost towns profit from the surroundings. The buildings at Hilltop are improved by having Shaw Peak as a backdrop. And the cemetery near Paradise, when I first saw it, was enhanced by the soft light of dusk and the presence of about twenty deer nearby.

Allow yourself time to explore and enjoy the Chiricahuas themselves, for if you see only the ghost towns you will have missed a great deal.

HILLTOP

To reach Hilltop, drive about 16 miles south from San Simon. Continue to the right where the road goes left to Portal, and then in 0.5 miles go right again. The road to Hilltop, 5 miles to the west, is the road marked as the way to Whitetail Canyon. Coming from the other direction, the turnoff is 4 miles north of Galeyville. The upper townsite of Hilltop is 0.5 miles up a road to the left just beyond the white house where the main road goes to the right. A truck can make it if the gates are not locked; if they are, the road makes for a brisk and scenic fifteen-minute uphill walk.

The original Hilltop was on the northwestern slope of Shaw Peak, a 7700-foot mountain in the Chiricahuas, but a tunnel about one mile long begun in 1917 enabled the town to be relocated at its present site, which was more convenient for transporting ore. The population of Hilltop at its peak was perhaps a hundred. A post office served the community from 1920 to 1945. Near the tunnel site up on the side of the mountain were a machine shop, bunkhouses, the superintendent's house, and other structures. In the canyon below, where the road from the outside still enters Hilltop, was the residential section where some families still live. One of the finest structures of Hilltop is the residence of the late Mr. and Mrs. Ralph Morrow (see Acknowledgments, page x). The home was originally the mine superintendent's up on the hillside and was moved down to the canyon in three sections. Only when you visit the upper townsite can you truly appreciate the difficulty of that task. On the main road into the Whitetail Creek area is one long residence that has been constructed by combining several small miners' cabins that were once at the upper townsite.

Principal points of interest: in the canyon, the Morrow house and other residences; on the hill, the one remaining shack and the many foundations; at the tunnel mouth, the buildings and mine equipment.

Hilltop — the mine superintendent's house, brought down in three sections from the upper townsite

Several of the upper townsite's quarters were moved and combined to create this attractive home at lower Hilltop.

Hilltop. Only one shack remains of the residential section of the upper site, but foundations and rubble abound.

One of two shacks that stand at the mouth of the Hilltop tunnel

Ore was poured down the chutes for transportation from Hilltop.

Paradise Cemetery

GALEYVILLE

Galeyville is 4 miles south of the intersection to Hilltop. Coming from the south, the turn-off up to Galeyville is 1 mile north of Paradise. Stop at the water tank and windmill.

Although Galeyville has no standing buildings, it does have its share of history. Pennsylvanian John Galey opened the Texas Mine and Smelter in Galeyville in 1881, but the mining operation lasted only two years; the smelter was carted off to Benson, over ninety miles away. But the end of mining was only the beginning of the town. Galeyville became a refuge for outlaws like Curly Bill Brocius and Johnny Ringo. Both worked an effective cattle rustling operation in the canyons of the area.

There isn't much in Galeyville now because many of the buildings were moved to nearby Paradise. A dilapidated wooden residence that stood just west of the windmill and water tank was torn down sometime between October 1978 and October 1979. The hole for the foundation marks the spot.

PARADISE

Paradise is 1 mile south of Galeyville and 5 miles west of Portal, Arizona.

Paradise was settled about 1901 with the establish-

ment of the Chiricahua Developing Company. The boom lasted only six years, but Paradise hung on, perhaps because of its beautiful location. The post office finally closed in 1943. There are several stories about the origin of the name. According to *Arizona Place Names,* George C. Walker and his bride honeymooned there and were in "Paradise."

Paradise's principal attraction is its cemetery, which is 1 mile east of the townsite on the road to Portal. In Paradise itself are several pleasant homes, one of which was built around the old jail. Another home was originally a saloon, but it has been so completely renovated that one would never know its past. The lone building that has the look of antiquity is an aging but well-preserved adobe structure on the west side of the road.

An eroding adobe building shares Paradise with modern homes and cottages.

The Dos Cabezas store, on the south side of the main highway to the Chiricahuas

DOS CABEZAS

Dos Cabezas is 15 miles southwest of Willcox on Arizona 186, and it is about 44 miles from Portal (near Paradise, Galeyville, and Hilltop).

Dos Cabezas (Spanish: "two heads") was named for the twin mountain peaks to the north. In 1851 the site was called Ewell Springs and served as a base camp for the commission surveying a boundary between the United States and Mexico. In 1857 the San Antonio and San Diego Stage Lines (the forerunner to the famous Butterfield Stage) built a station at the site. Its ruins are still visible.

Gold and silver caused the town of Dos Cabezas to develop about 1878 and prosper well into the twentieth century.

Visit the cemetery on the right side of the highway from Willcox just before you enter the town. In Dos Cabezas itself, notice the bleached adobe ruins on the highway and several wooden and

Dos Cabezas's adobe buildings, unlike most of the roofless adobe ruins in Arizona, have as yet retained their white plaster.

The headframe and headquarters of the Elma Mine, near Dos Cabezas, taken from a miner's cabin

adobe buildings. One street south of the highway are the old post office and, next door, the foundations of the old stage depot.

A dirt road heading north from the center of Dos Cabezas goes past the old school to the Mascot Mine, 3.4 miles from Dos Cabezas, which has a few decaying buildings and rubble remaining. The better-preserved Elma Mine is 3.5 miles north of the Mascot on the north side of the Dos Cabezas range. Consult the Dos Cabezas 15′ topographic map. A truck can reach the Mascot, but a four-wheel drive vehicle is essential for the Elma.

CAPSULE SUMMARY

(In order of importance of sites)

MAJOR SITES

Dos Cabezas — about a dozen buildings and an interesting cemetery

Hilltop — several residences (still in use), many foundations, good remains of a mine

MINOR SITES

Paradise — picturesque cemetery; not much of the original town remains

Galeyville — no buildings, but a pretty spot

TRIP SUGGESTIONS

This area requires two days from Tucson if you are really to enjoy the townsites and the beautiful Chiricahua Mountains. Several possible itineraries can be followed because this section can be joined to any of the Tombstone Territory trips to make a complete southeastern Arizona ghost town tour.

Portal, Arizona, is the logical place to stay overnight, and the Cave Creek Ranch and other places there offer pleasant accommodations at the doorway to the Chiricahuas. You'll see wildlife in abundance — deer, skunk, javelina, squirrel, and many species of birds.

WARNING: In winter or severe weather, the road across the Chiricahuas from Portal to Dos Cabezas may be closed or hazardous. Inquire at Portal or at the Chiricahua National Monument.

TRIP 1: Hilltop, Galeyville, Paradise, and Dos Cabezas

Drive east from Tucson on I-10 through Willcox and on to San Simon, a distance of 130 miles. From there go 26 miles south to Portal. Driving time from Tucson to Portal is about three hours. You can visit Hilltop, Galeyville, and Paradise en route to Portal. I'd suggest two to three hours at Hilltop, but Galeyville and Paradise probably will require only about forty-five minutes altogether. There is a general store in Portal for food and supplies. On the second day, drive to Dos Cabezas by taking the 22-mile road across the Chiricahuas — it's slow but well maintained and the scenery is quite beautiful. You might want to visit the Chiricahua National Monument. Northwest of the monument 18 miles is Dos Cabezas, on the way to Willcox. Before you get there, a turnoff heads to Ft. Bowie National Historical Site. From Dos Cabezas, you can head toward Tombstone Territory sites such as Cochise, Pearce, or Tombstone.

TRIP 2: Dos Cabezas, Paradise, Galeyville, and Hilltop

By reversing trip 1, you can see all the Chiricahua ghost towns by early the second day and go from Portal through Douglas, Arizona, and over to Bisbee. If you plan your trip for the second Sunday of the month, you could even head north to I-10 from Portal through Rodeo, New Mexico, and on to Shakespeare, New Mexico. Shakespeare is about 60 miles from Portal and is one of the West's best preserved genuine ghost towns. Only on the second Sunday of each month is it open to visitors.

TOPOGRAPHIC MAP INFORMATION
FOR CHAPTER ELEVEN
THE CHIRICAHUA GHOSTS
(For map reading assistance, consult Appendix A, page 127)

Town	Topo Map Name	Size	Importance*
Hilltop	Chiricahua Peak	15′	3
Galeyville	Portal, AZ–Rodeo, NM	15′	2
Paradise	Portal, AZ–Rodeo, NM	15′	3
Dos Cabezas	Dos Cabezas	15′	3

*1 — essential to find and/or enjoy site to the fullest
2 — helpful but not essential
3 — unnecessary for finding and enjoying site

APPENDIXES

APPENDIX A:
Reading Topographic Maps

A topographic map is a representation of natural and manmade features of a portion of the earth plotted to a specific scale. It shows locations and shapes of mountains, valleys, rivers, and lakes as well as principal works of man.

For the ghost town enthusiast, the topographic map (or "topo" or "quad") is a particularly valuable aid in locating towns in remote areas, determining where mines were near those towns, and noting what buildings or ruins were at the site when the map was made. Topos are more valuable than highway maps because they are so much more detailed. Nevertheless, some topos are more essential than others (although all are useful); in many cases the maps in this book are all you will need for outings. But be certain to check the Topographic Map Information pages for the various chapters before you go.

15 Minute and 7-1/2 Minute

The two map sizes you will most frequently encounter are 15 minute and 7½ minute maps. There are 360 degrees of latitude and longitude to the earth and 60 minutes to each degree. A 15′ map covers one-fourth of a degree of latitude or longitude; sixteen 15′ maps cover one degree of latitude **and** one degree of longitude. A 7½′ map, which is larger in size than a 15′ map, actually covers only one-fourth the area of a 15′ map.

As a result, the 7½′ is much more detailed and

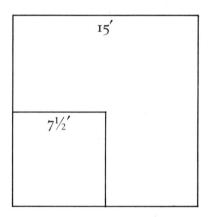

usually far more helpful to the ghost town hunter. In a 15′ map, one inch represents about one mile; in a 7½′, one inch represents about 2,000 feet. Since a 7½′ map covers such a small area, you must buy several to cover a part of the state filled with ghost towns if you want topos for them all. For example, I have fourteen for the Prescott area. But if you will consult the Topographic Map Information for Chapter One, page 21, you will discover that only two topos are essential since you have this book; five more are very helpful but not essential.

Generally, the 15′ maps are the older topos, for the U.S. Geological Survey has been replacing many of the 15′ maps with four 7½′ maps when new surveys are made. Nevertheless, the older maps are still quite valuable, since a topo from 1947 will show what was there decades ago, so the real adventurer can scour the area for nearly vanished roads and decaying foundations that are not apparent to the casual visitor.

is chosen because of a prominent feature, either natural or manmade, on that map.

Distinguishing Characteristics

The primary feature of a topographic map that is unfamiliar to the average person is the brown contour lines that extend throughout the map. These show steepness of slope. Quite simply, where the contour lines are close together the grade is steep; where they are far apart the land is fairly level. You have, no doubt, had the experience when traveling a back road of following the gently curving line on the highway map only to discover that it is a dangerous, mountainous route. The topo clearly shows the terrain, so you should have a much clearer picture of the road ahead.

Another unfamiliar feature is the presence of red squares crisscrossing the map. They are particularly helpful, since each is one square mile, called a "section." Not all areas, however, have been surveyed for square mile sections. The area around Crown King (see page 16) is such an area.

The final unfamiliar feature of the topographic map is the presence of numbers like "R. 1 W." and "T. 10 N." These refer to the map's location relative to the initial point of reference of the Arizona maps, the Gila and Salt River Meridian (north and south) and the Gila and Salt River Baseline (east and west). The latter should be familiar to all Phoenix residents — Baseline Road. The Meridian intersects the Baseline south of Avondale at a spot about twelve miles west of Phoenix, approximately at the point where the Salt River enters the Gila River. A monument marks the spot.

The notations R. 1 W. and T. 10 N. indicate a place in the first **range** west of the Meridian and ten **townships** north of the Baseline. A township-range is an area six miles by six miles usually subdivided into 36 sections of one square mile each. In R. 1 W. and T. 10 N. are the ghost towns of Crown King and Oro Belle.

I suggest buying a map for an area that you wish to visit and studying it carefully. On the margins of the topo is such information as the scale, showing distances; the date the map was made; the location of the quadrangle of which this map is a part; the difference between true and magnetic north when the map was made; and very importantly, the names of the eight maps that border the map you have. The name of the map, incidentally,

Availability

Topographic maps are available at many blueprint shops, hunters' or hikers' supply stores, and some bookstores. When in doubt, look in the Yellow Pages under "Maps." While you are purchasing the maps, you should also request (free of charge) an index, which shows all the topographic maps available in Arizona; and a topographic symbols sheet, which details the various lines, colors, and symbols used in the maps. If you know well in advance which maps you will need, you can cut the cost of the maps almost in half by ordering directly from:

Branch of Distribution
U.S. Geological Survey
Box 25286, Federal Center
Denver, Colorado 80225

A handy brochure that I consulted for this appendix is "Topographic Maps" by Theodore D. Steger, available without charge at some U.S. Geological Survey offices.

Comparing Maps

The illustration above is a portion of a highway map of Arizona showing the location of Crown King in the Bradshaw Mountains southeast of Prescott. About all you can tell for certain about Crown King is that it is twelve miles from Cleator and fourteen from Goodwin. What you cannot tell is that the road from Cleator is quite mountainous and that the road to Goodwin is not for passenger cars at all. In fact, there is no town at Goodwin, only a site. A highway map is perfectly suited for getting you around Arizona on major roads, but it is not suited for ghost town hunting on the back roads.

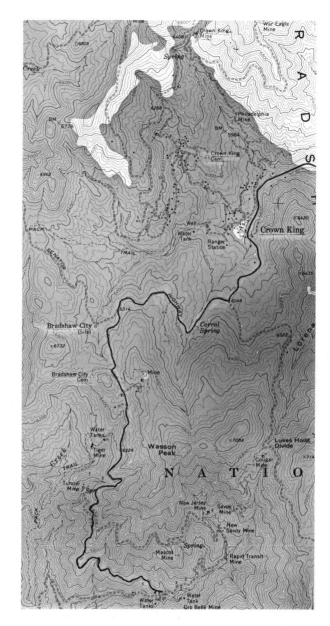

A portion of the 15′ Crown King topographic map, above, for the same vicinity as that light area on the highway map, shows an area of about four miles north to south and two miles east to west. Notice the contour lines and how clearly they show the mountainous terrain. In addition to the town of Crown King, where you can actually see the position of the main buildings, you can also determine the route to the Crown King Mine and to the town of Oro Belle (the route to Crown King and Oro Belle is darkened for emphasis). You can also see other mines in the area and the locations and altitudes for such natural features as Wasson Peak.

The 7½′ map of the same location (right) shows the area magnified four times and in considerably more detail. Several more mines are indicated as well as more natural features. But there are even more important additions: the Crown King cemetery, the Bradshaw City site, the Bradshaw City cemetery, and the placement of buildings at Oro Belle. When I visited Oro Belle, I had only the 15′ topo and so went right past the Bradshaw City cemetery, oblivious to its existence.

The map for Chapter One of this book (see page xiv) includes the same areas as these topos. Coupled with the directions included in the individual entries, this map is more useful than a highway map but far less detailed than topographic maps. For the person who wishes to see more at a site than the obvious and to explore more of the area to get a real feeling for what once was there, the topographic map is an irreplaceable aid.

APPENDIX B: Glossary of Frequently-Used Mining Terms

ADIT: A horizontal or nearly horizontal entrance to a mine; a tunnel.

ARRASTRA: A Spanish word for a circular rock-crushing device, usually powered by mules or oxen.

HEADFRAME: The vertical apparatus over a mine shaft that has cables to be lowered down the shaft for the raising of ore; sometimes called a "gallows frame."

MILL: A building in which rock is crushed in order to extricate minerals; usually constructed on the side of a hill — hence, a "gravity-feed" mill.

PLACER: A waterborne deposit of sand or gravel containing heavier minerals like gold that have been eroded from their original bedrock and concentrated as small particles that can be washed out.

SHAFT: A vertical or nearly vertical opening into the earth for mining.

SMELTER: A building or complex in which material is melted so as to separate impurities from pure metal.

STAMP MILL: A machine that pulverizes ore by means of heavy hammers or pestles, called "stamps."

TAILINGS: Waste or refuse left after milling is complete; sometimes used more generally to include waste dumps.

WASTE DUMP: Waste rock that comes out of the mine; rock that is not of sufficient value to warrant milling.

APPENDIX C: Pronunciation Guide

Many westerners and speakers of Spanish may find this appendix unnecessary. The pronunciations have been checked with natives to the areas in most cases. Foreign words, most of which are Spanish, are given in their anglicized form.

Agua Fria — ah-wa-*free*-uh

Alto — *awl*-toh

Amerind — *am*-er-ind

Arivaca — air-uh-*vah*-kah

Arrastre — uh-*rass*-truh

Bouse — rhymes with "house"

Brunckow — *brunn*-kow

Cerbat — *ser*-bat

Cerro Colorado — *sare*-roh (Colorado)

Chiricahua — cheer-uh-*kah*-wah

Cleator — *clee*-ter

Cordes — *cord*-ess

Dos Cabezas — dose-ka-*bay*-suss

Dragoon — drag-*oon*

Duquesne — doo-*kayne*

Duval — doo-*vall* (locals sometimes say *doo*-val)

El Recreo — ell-*reck*-ray-oh

Gattrell — *gat*-trull

Gila — *hee*-luh

Grosvenors — *groe*-ven-orz

Harqua Hala — *har*-kwuh-*hay*-luh

Hassayampa — hah-see-*yamp*-uh

Huachuca — wah-*chew*-kuh

Hualapai — *wall*-uh-pie

Jerez — *hair*-ess

La Osa — lah-*oh*-suh

Lochiel — loh-*keel*

Madera — mah-*dare*-uh

Mogollon — *muggy*-own

Mohave — moh-*hah*-vee

Mowry — *mow* (as in "cow")-ree

Nogales — noh-*gah*-less

Ookilsipava — oo-kill-sih-*pah*-vah
(pronunciation approximate)

Oro Blanco — *ore*-oh-*blon*-koh

Patagonia — pat-uh-*go*-nee-uh

Peña Blanca — *pay*-nyuh-*blan*-kah

Picacho — pih-*kah*-choe

Pimeria Alta — pee-mair-*ee*-uh *awl*-tuh

Placer — *plass*-er

Placerita — plass-er-*ee*-tuh

Plomo — *ploh*-moh

Plomosa — pluh-*moh*-suh

Prescott — *press*-cut (preferred over *press*-cott)

Sahuarita — sour-*ee*-tah

Salero — sah-*lare*-oh

Salome — suh-*loam*, not suh-*loam*-ee

San Simon — san see-*moan*

Schieffelin — *sheff*-lin

Schuylkill — *skoo*-kl

Socorro — suh-*corr*-oh

Sonoita — sun-*oy*-tuh

Sonora — suh-*norr*-uh

Swansea — *swan*-see

Tritle — *try*-tl

Tubac — *too*-bock

Tumacacori — toom-uh-*cock*-uh-ree

Venezia — ven-*ee*-see-uh

Wikieup — *wick*-ee-up

Yavapai — *yav*-uh-pie

APPENDIX D: Photographing Ghost Towns

Consider one certainty: film is cheap compared to gasoline. Consider one probability: you may never return to a particular ghost town, and even if you do, it **will not** look the same the second time. For these reasons, take along a camera and plenty of film.

The Camera

Any old camera is certainly better than no camera on a ghost town outing, but the person who insists, "I can take just as good a picture with my pocket camera as I could with a fancy camera" simply isn't correct. If the pictures which that person takes please him, that is all that really matters. But better cameras do take better pictures because their lenses are more precisely ground and because they are infinitely more versatile with their varying shutter speeds and apertures. With the advent of "automatic" single lens reflex cameras, the quality photograph is now virtually as easy to take as the "pocket" photograph is.

In suggesting what camera to use, professionals will likely give the nod to what are called medium- and large-format cameras. But the most popular quality camera on the market, and perhaps the most practical, is the 35mm single lens reflex (SLR) camera. As it is so popular and relatively affordable, and as it is my personal choice, I will suggest equipment based on an SLR system. An SLR allows you to get excellent photographs with the initial investment as well as add lenses and other accessories when you become more sophisticated and demanding with your camera.

The Accessories

- In addition to the 50mm lens usually standard with an SLR, the most important lens for ghost-towning is a 28mm or 35mm wide angle lens. This lens is particularly valuable for showing interiors of buildings and for conveying the look of the overall site.

- A third lens that often allows the photographer the only real look at a site (e.g. if it is closed to visitors or on a distant cliff) is the telephoto, a lens of 135mm or more. You might consider a zoom lens for the same purpose. Purists claim that a zoom does not give as clear an image as a fixed lens, but it is tremendously versatile. Many photographs in this book were taken with a zoom lens.

- Use an ultraviolet (UV) haze filter or a skylight filter on any of your lenses for two reasons: they protect the lens itself from damage, and they correct for excessive bluishness in the outdoors.

- If you don't have macro capabilities on a lens, buy a close-up lens set. It's very inexpensive and allows you to photograph all sorts of details at a site such as buttons, hinges, tin, glass, and ornamental iron.

- A tripod permits low-light photography, such as in mines, interiors of buildings, and dawn and dusk photos. It also permits you to be in your own pictures if your camera has a self-timer.

- For those occasions when a tripod is too slow, too bulky, or too heavy, carry an electronic flash. I have a small pocket-sized flash on hikes, and a large thyristor-type flash stays in my case in the car.

- Speaking of cases — a camera bag or case is an essential piece of equipment, not an accessory. You will be driving over miles of back roads, and dust is a camera's worst enemy. Most bags do an acceptable job of keeping out dust; aluminum cases, such as a Halliburton, are virtually dustproof but are expensive. Incidentally, in addition to keeping your camera away from dust, also keep it and your spare film out of prolonged direct sunlight or heat, such as baking in the car for hour after hour. A moisture-proof pouch kept in your cooler is a wise choice.

Film

Slide film has advantages over print film for ghost town enthusiasts. It is cheaper per frame, and it is easier to show your pictures with a projector than to pass them around to friends. In addition, since your slide **is** the processed film itself, what you see is what you took; no error should be made in cropping by the photo lab, a problem which occurs often with print film. Finally, those especially good slides can be made into prints of very good quality. Print film has the advantage that it is a better quality print than a print from a slide, and naturally, print film does not require the expense of a projector.

I prefer Ektachrome over Kodachrome because the color is more true to the actual scene; Kodachrome gives the more splendid, more dramatic results because of its emphasis on reds and browns, but I find it a bit dishonest — often the photographs are more beautiful than the scenes themselves were. My purpose, as I see it, is to record the sites as accurately as possible. If your purpose is different, choose your film accordingly. In addition, Ektachrome is available in a much wider range of film speeds. All color photographs and several of the black and whites in this book were originally Ektachrome slides.

How much film should you have with you? This varies enormously depending upon your desire to record the site. When I was in Ruby, Arizona, I took about 175 photos. A friend with an excellent camera took about 40. He and I were both happy with our results. For a normal full day's outing, I take along four to six rolls of 36 exposure film. I very rarely use it all, but then I have never run out of film at a site two hours' drive from the nearest town, either.

Suggestions for Technique

- Perhaps the first rule is: know your camera and its capabilities by studying the manual and experimenting with the camera. You might also be wise to buy an inexpensive book on photography to learn about techniques like backlighting, bracketing, multiple exposure, and others.

- If your reason for taking a camera is to show others and remind yourself what the ghost town looks like, try to take some pictures that give a feeling of the totality of the site. You can do this by either taking pictures from a hill or by including in several pictures a common reference point, such as a church steeple, smelter stack, or large ruin. Then, when showing your pictures, you can help the viewer get a better image of the town by saying "just north of that smelter stack" or "to the west of that same building is this adobe ruin," and so on.

- While looking at the large — the headframes of mines, the tailings, the buildings — don't overlook the small — weathered wood, a rusted hinge — which may offer the most intriguing and personally satisfying photos. Cemeteries, for example, often contain many details worth examining.

- If you have Jim and Barbara Sherman's *Ghost Towns of Arizona* or any other text that includes historical photographs, it's interesting to take pictures from the same spot to try to duplicate the historical photograph's perspective to see how the site has changed. Then photograph the picture from the book and include it among your slides (most old photographs are in the public domain and are reprinted out of courtesy, not copyright).

- Although dawn and dusk generally offer the most dramatic photographic possibilities, those times are not the most practical for people taking full-day tours. The fact is, good photographs can be taken with a quality camera under almost any conditions. Some of my favorite photographs of ghost towns were taken on dismal, gloomy days; those pictures convey a desolation and abandonment that sunshine would only have abated.

APPENDIX E: Driving and Walking in Arizona

Survival tips are far too important to be relegated to an appendix of a ghost town book. Your local civil defense agency should have a pamphlet on the subject, and several good books have been written for the hiker and for the four-wheel drive owner.

The following guidelines are **not** intended to replace definitive books on survival techniques.

General Suggestions

1. Let someone know exactly where you're going. Show them on a map.
2. Have a good map with you.
3. Have a compass and know how to use it.
4. Have a snakebite kit and know how to use it.

5. Have plenty of water with you, at least one gallon per person per day. Ice is also advisable in case of snake or insect bites.

6. Have the necessary tools (see "Your Car," below).

7. Have the necessary survival gear (see "Survival Kit," right).

8. If your car breaks down and you are many miles from help, you are probably best off staying with the vehicle, especially in the desert heat. Use your signaling devices when appropriate (see "Survival Kit," right).

9. Above all, STAY CALM. Don't do anything until you have logically evaluated an emergency situation.

You

Know your limitations. The desert or mountainside is no place to determine if you are in good physical shape. If you require some sort of medication, be certain that there is an adequate supply in the survival kit. Wear comfortable clothing, including a hat, and shoes designed for walking; boots are best. Carry a watch (and a compass, canteen, and knife if you're walking any distance from the car). Know the temperature extremes in the area during a given time of year and have clothes in the car in anticipation of those extremes.

Your Car

Make sure your car is in excellent mechanical condition before you go anywhere on the back roads. Especially check tires, radiator hoses, belts, and all fluid levels. Check that the spare tire is inflated properly. Carry a set of tools, spare belts, a good jack, at least one quart of oil, fuses, jumper cables, fire extinguisher, electrical tape, duct tape, baling wire or an equivalent, flares, a shovel, a gas siphon, and perhaps a can of Fix-a-Flat for temporary tire repairs. If yours is a four-wheel drive vehicle and you're going deep into the back country, you need to carry a lot more. Consult your manual or a book on the subject.

Survival Kit

The following, adapted from a kit recommended in a Civil Defense brochure "Your Plan for Survival," should be in your car at all times:

1. Swiss Army knife
2. Waterproof matches
3. Good compass with a protected face
4. "Thunderer" whistle
5. Signaling mirror
6. Magnifying glass — for starting fires
7. Large-eyed needles and linen thread
8. Parachute silk, bright orange — for shelter, protecting the face in sandstorms, straining water, and signaling
9. Aluminum foil
10. Water purification tablets
11. Large orange balloons — for water storage or signaling
12. Candles
13. Razor blade
14. Pencil and note paper — for leaving notes or marking a trail
15. Adhesive tape
16. Small first aid kit
17. Fish hooks — for setting snares
18. Assorted nails
19. Snakebite kit
20. A sharp belt knife
21. Parachute-type tow rope
22. Blankets

All of the above items, except for the last two, fit compactly into a container about the size of an overnight bag.

Remember: have plenty of water. All of those cold cans of soft drinks will not be what you'll want or need if you get stranded.

BIBLIOGRAPHY

The two principal sources for this book are:

Granger, Byrd H. *Will C. Barnes' Arizona Place Names*. Tucson: University of Arizona Press, 1960.

Sherman, James E. and Barbara H. *Ghost Towns of Arizona*. Norman: University of Oklahoma Press, 1969.

Other sources consulted include:

Arizona, April 1916.

Arizona Republic, various issues.

Barnes, Will C. *Arizona Place Names*. Tucson: University of Arizona Press, 1935.

Carter, William. *Ghost Towns of the West*. Menlo Park, California: Lane Publishing Co., 1978.

Florin, Lambert. *Arizona Ghost Towns*. Seattle: Superior Publishing Co., 1971.

Silver Belt, 21 January 1926.

Spude, Robert L., and Paher, Stanley W. *Central Arizona Ghost Towns*. Las Vegas: Nevada Publications, 1978.

Steger, Theodore. *Topographic Maps*. U.S. Geological Survey, U.S. Government Printing Office, 1978.

Way, W. J. "Jack." *Ghosts and Ghost Towns*. Copyright W. John Way, 1966.

Weis, Norman D. *Ghost Towns of the Northwest*. Caldwell, Idaho: The Caxton Printers, Ltd., 1977.

————. *Helldorados, Ghosts and Camps of the Old Southwest*. Caldwell, Idaho: The Caxton Printers, Ltd., 1977.

Wolle, Muriel Sibell. *The Bonanza Trail*. Chicago: The Swallow Press, Inc., 1953.

MAPS

Arizona Office of Tourism Multipurpose and Outdoor Recreational Facilities Maps: a series of seven.

United States Geological Survey: topographic maps of the area.

MISCELLANEOUS BROCHURES

From: The Vulture Mine
The Cochise Hotel
The Tombstone, Arizona, Chamber of Commerce
Pioneer Arizona
The Wickenburg, Arizona, Chamber of Commerce

INDEX

Pages numbers in italics indicate photographs.